BEWARE of CAT

BEWARE of CAT

and Other Encounters of a Letter Carrier

VINCENT WYCKOFF

BOREALIS
BOOKS

Borealis Books is an imprint of the Minnesota Historical Society Press.
www.borealisbooks.org

The Minnesota Historical Society Press is a member of the Association
of American University Presses.

Manufactured in the United States of America

10 9 8 7 6 5 4 3 2 1

∞ The paper used in this publication meets the minimum requirements of the
American National Standard for Information Sciences—Permanence for
Printed Library Materials, ANSI Z39.48-1984.

International Standard Book Number

ISBN 13: 978-1-68134-075-3

Library of Congress Cataloging-in-Publication Data

Wyckoff, Vincent, 1952–

   Beware of cat and other encounters of a letter carrier / Vincent Wyckoff.
      p. cm.
   ISBN-13: 978-1-68134-075-3 (cloth : alk. paper)
   1. Letter carriers. I. Title.

   HE6241.W93 2007
   383'.492—dc22

                                                          2006035273

For MacKenzie Wyckoff—
this is what your grandpa did

CONTENTS

ACKNOWLEDGMENTS

For her encouraging words at the outset and critical feedback throughout, I want to thank my good friend, Martha Anderson. A special thank you to my former classmate and faithful writing group member, Paula Zuhlsdorf, who taught me how to splash some color into the black-and-white printed word. Later, Luaina Lewis spent hours proofreading my work, giving me the confidence to send it out into the big, bad world.

The staff at Borealis Books has been outstanding. My editor, Ann Regan, brought great skill and sensitivity to the project. Many thanks to Greg Britton and Alison Vandenberg.

I want to recognize my fellow letter carriers at the Nokomis Post Office, whose integrity and work ethic never take a day off. I'm proud to work beside them. Of course, this book would not be possible without the wonderful folks living on Route 17. It has been a pleasure delivering their mail each day and an honor to know them. These are their stories, and while I've attempted to relate them as accurately as memory allows, it should be noted that every writer is a storyteller first.

I also want to thank my best friend and wife, Sybil, for listening to my mail-delivering escapades throughout the years. She often commented that I needed to write these stories down, but I didn't take her good advice until the day she asked about a particular character from a tale I had related years earlier. I barely remembered the incident, and the fear of losing these stories inspired me to get them down on paper. Thanks, Syb.

≡✉≡

ONE EVENING SEVERAL YEARS AGO, Sybil and I invited a few friends over for dinner. Our oldest son, Sam, was finishing up high school, and I had recently noticed his less-than-exuberant response whenever the topic of college arose. In our house, from the time the kids were old enough to understand the words, the discussion had always been about *when* you go to college, not *if*.

Gathered at the dinner table were some interesting conversationalists, so as host I took the opportunity to ask a question that I hoped would spark a discussion about furthering one's education and reaching for goals and dreams.

"If you could have any career imaginable," I asked, "with no concern about how much money you earn, or how much education it requires, what would you choose to do for a living, and why?"

One by one I directed the question around the table. Some of the answers were downright startling, creating lively rounds of laughter and conversation. There was the insurance agent who saw himself as a classical musician, and a nurse who dreamed of being a doctor working with Doctors Without Borders. A corporate communications executive said she would have been a puppeteer. "I've always loved the Muppets," she added.

Sam listened and laughed along with the rest of us. I wasn't sure my little exercise had fulfilled the intended purpose until we reached the end. When the laughter died down, Sam spoke up, directing the question my way. "How about you, Dad? What would you do for a living?" he asked. "Would you still choose to deliver mail?"

Everyone looked at me, and I found that providing an answer was no simple task. I had been too busy working and raising a family to ponder such questions. For years my wife and I had concentrated on helping the kids grow up strong and healthy and motivated, and I hadn't thought about my own dreams for a while.

"You know, Sam, I've always wanted to be an author. If I had the opportunity, and a chance to take some classes, I think I'd sit down and write a book."

"Well then, why don't you do it? You're always telling me that I can be whatever I want. If your dream is to be an author, to write a book, then you should do it."

So here it is, Sam, with a nod of gratitude.

BEWARE of CAT

The Red Piñata

After delivering mail on the same route for over fifteen years, I've become something of a fixture in the lives of more than five hundred residents in a quiet neighborhood in South Minneapolis. I know all their first and last names, including the children's, and I can recite every name in every house as I drive through the route.

I learn much more than just names, however, while delivering the mail. Stacks of handwritten cards show that someone is celebrating a birthday or anniversary. Certified letters from the irs clearly signal an investigation. Newspapers from other towns reveal a patron's origins. I know who receives X-rated magazines, and for a time I delivered love letters to a woman from an inmate in federal prison. The explicit artwork penciled on the envelopes was the clue.

Change-of-address forms show where someone is moving to, or where a new family is coming from. I'm aware of divorces and separations, when a child is born or somebody passes away. I've even attended some of their memorial services. Of course, I know every single dog on my route, the good ones as well as the bad.

Years ago, when still a substitute carrier, I noticed a warning sign on an open porch: Beware of Cat! I grinned at the snarling animal etched on the sign as I put mail in the box. Not until I turned to leave did I notice the huge feline watching me from a shadowed corner of the porch. With its back arched, the cat spat at me, showing off gleaming canines. I lunged for the steps, but he caught me halfway down. He clawed his way up my legs and latched onto my mail satchel as I ran for the next house. He finally let go, but then strutted along the perimeter of the yard to ensure I had no plans to return. After all these years, I'm sure that cat is long gone, but I'll never forget that house.

While it's possible to learn many details of people's lives from the mail they receive, most of what I've discovered has come from talking to people. It can't be helped. Walk through someone's life once a day, year after year after year, and you're bound to learn a few things.

My relationships with several patrons are almost like those within an extended family, and I know other carriers enjoy similar connections. As coworkers we share many of our experiences from the route; however, out of respect to the patrons, we keep some stories, as well as people's names, to ourselves.

One of the more important lessons I've learned, and the most incredible to me, is how many everyday heroes are walking around out there: unassuming folks who have accomplished amazing feats with little fanfare or acclaim. Take all the war veterans, for instance. On my route lives a man who landed on

Iwo Jima. His old unit holds a reunion every year, and he tells me how the few remaining survivors still shed tears when the reminiscing begins. I've talked to Korean War vets and listened to stories from veterans of both gulf wars.

One fellow on my route fought in Vietnam. He is a quiet, modest man with a tidy little house and a loving family. It was years before he finally talked to me about being drafted and becoming a machine gunner in the infantry. He told me how, over just a few months' time, his whole unit was killed off and replaced by new recruits, many of whom didn't make it home themselves. He was shot in the neck and barely survived. Now the vertebrae in his upper back are fusing together, twisting his head and neck painfully. The Veterans Administration won't help him because he can't prove his wounds caused the problem. The truly amazing aspect of the story is his lack of bitterness. Unable to drive anymore, he goes to work every day on the bus and always greets me with a smile and a wave when I see him.

Not all of my patrons' stories evoke compassion, however. Another fellow lost his wife to cancer at a very young age. For the last few months of her life, a nurse spent several hours every day with her to make her as comfortable as possible. One day, I accidentally spotted the husband and nurse in a compromising position on the couch. I wasn't surprised when they became engaged just two months after the wife died.

Above all, I particularly admire those people who quietly go about living their lives, raising families (a heroic effort in itself) while trying to do the right thing by others, especially those folks who struggle with emotional, mental, or physical disabilities. They go to work every day at menial jobs, pay their bills, and find peace and enjoyment in the little victories and rewards of life.

With so much time on the same assignment, I've seen children go off for their first day of kindergarten—and years later I've attended their high school graduation parties. In South Minneapolis, these summertime celebrations are often centered on a backyard barbeque. Colorful helium-filled balloons are a common decorating motif: blue and orange for Washburn High, burgundy and gold for Roosevelt, and black and orange for South.

=✉=

A FEW YEARS AGO I witnessed the preparations for a slightly different graduation party. The Anayas, a family of recent immigrants from Central America, lived together in a tiny one-bedroom house: a young boy and girl, their parents, and their grandmother. The boy, and occasionally the grandmother, met me at the door to get the mail. They never said anything, just nodded and smiled. I figured it was a language thing, because sometimes I offered a "gracias," or "buenos dias," and they giggled while responding with a phrase totally incomprehensible to me.

One day the front door was wide open. I couldn't help but see inside. A mix-and-match array of kitchen chairs, stools, straight-backed wooden seats, and folding chairs neatly lined the walls of the small front room. Dozens of pages of crayon artwork, finger paintings, and elementary worksheets of ABCs were taped to the walls. A bright red piñata, shaped like a bunny, hung from the light fixture. Salsa music played softly in the background. Then the little boy came running through the house to meet me.

"Are you having a party?" I asked.

The grin on his face threatened to consume him. His big brown eyes shimmered and sparkled. "Later," he replied, bouncing up and down as he reached for the mail. I think that was the first word of English I ever heard from him.

"Is it a birthday party?" I asked, thinking his excitement was due to the presents he would soon be opening.

But he shook his head. "My sister," he said.

"It's your sister's birthday?"

Again he shook his head. I thought the kid would burst. "My sister, she is done from kindergarten!" he exclaimed.

I smiled and turned to leave. It seemed they were making a mighty big deal out of passing kindergarten, but maybe it was a big deal for the little girl. After all, she was the one who had gone off to school all alone in a strange new country. She hadn't even spoken the language all that well.

As I reached the foot of their stairs, I realized her little brother, who could not possibly understand her accomplishment, was showing the joy and pride he sensed in his parents and grandmother. His sister was launched into this new world, and he would soon follow. I glanced back to see him standing in the doorway, the bright red piñata swaying in the breeze behind him.

A Splendid Day

There is no question that delivering mail in the deep freeze of a Minnesota January is difficult. The thing to remember about an Upper Midwest winter, however, is that it's a familiar, known entity, and while it may be relentless, it is at least honest and straightforward. Letter carriers will forget a snowstorm with a foot of snow within a couple of weeks. We brag about delivering mail in twenty-five-degrees-below-zero temperatures; wind chills must reach sixty below to be remembered until the end of the season. These hardships are expected in the winter, and we slug it out with felt liners and Vibram soles on the ice, while piling on layers of wool and cotton flannel against the cold.

It's the *length* of our winters that make them so demoralizing. Well into April my fellow letter carriers maintain hunched-over shuffles, with fur hats and woolen scarves always near at hand. By then, the snow cover is receding grudgingly, like a bully grown tired of the game. But we know not to let our guard down, for there's a deceptively brutal day each spring that sneaks down out of the far North Country to smack us with a wintry sucker punch.

The day begins in a harmless fashion, with nothing more than a light drizzle. Maybe a little rain from time to time, but mostly just a cold mist hanging in the air, a continuous cloak of dampness to walk through. Temperatures hover around the freezing point all day. At the end of a block, and sometimes between houses, an icy wind off the Canadian snowpack pokes and prods at the layers of clothing. After several hours of this, tendrils of Arctic air finger their way through coats and sweaters, meeting up with the freezing rain that inevitably finds its way beneath collars and gloves. It doesn't matter how many layers we wear, or what the fabric. Eventually, the cold wins out.

Carriers plod back to the station at the end of their routes, pulling off wet clothing, clapping hands together to thaw frozen fingers. There's no need to commiserate, no use seeking sympathy, for every carrier has just endured the same miserable day. Slumped on your stool, exhausted, you look around to take stock of your comrades.

"Where's Joe?"

"Not back yet."

If the missing carrier is older, or has recently been sick or injured, you may get some volunteers to go back out with you to help. A supervisor might ask a younger carrier with less seniority. These are the days we truly dread, and it seems that Old Man Winter relishes this one last laugh at our expense every spring.

But now we had put even April behind us for another year.

It was the first truly mild day of summer, with the sun resting warm on my face. My stride opened up, and my neck and shoulder kinks began to loosen. A soft breeze out of the south carried the first taste of humidity, the first aromas of a reawakening Earth. Even the mail volume was lighter on this delightful day.

Near the end of my route, I spotted Mr. Harris standing on the city sidewalk looking up at the bare treetops. I was earlier than usual, so I sauntered over to talk. Mr. Harris had been retired for more years than I had been on the route, and I encountered him regularly working in his yard. He wasn't the greatest talker, however, and we never got beyond the usual greetings and brief discussions of the weather. Sometimes, like today, I saw him slowly walking around the block. He was very old and stopped often to rest.

"Hello, Mr. Harris," I called as I approached. He gave me just the briefest glance, then returned to his inspection of the treetops. Nothing could spoil my mood, though, so I put on a big smile and asked, "How are you? Isn't this a lovely day?"

"My bird escaped," he replied. I wasn't sure I had heard him correctly, but then he added, "He must have opened the cage door by himself. He's a real smart one, you know."

I followed his gaze up into the treetops. "He escaped? What kind of bird is it?"

"A parakeet. He's bright green and yellow. No bigger than your fist, but real smart. Smarter than most people I know," he added, finally looking at me.

Ignoring his sarcasm, I asked, "He can fly? I thought they clip their wings or something."

"Don't you believe it! That's what they tell you, but those little devils can fly. Not very far, mind you, but you can bet they'll take off if they get out of the cage. And fast? Turn your back for a second, and they're gone."

I looked down the street, scanning trees and bushes, wondering what we'd do even if we got lucky and spotted him. Suddenly, the old man let go with a piercing whistle. I jumped back, almost dropping a handful of mail, and the hair on the back of my neck stood up. The tremolo echoed through the neighborhood.

"That's what he sounds like," he said, peering through the leafless trees like a squirrel hunter searching for dinner.

"Green and yellow, you say?"

"Yup. He's small, but real smart. If you see him, just whistle like I showed you. He might come land on your shoulder. But remember, that little guy is mighty clever."

"Sure. I'll keep an eye out." Setting off again on my rounds, I called back to him, "Good luck, Mr. Harris."

I was glad to get away, but I felt bad for the old guy. He wasn't the type to admit it, but it was obvious that bird meant a lot to him. The least I could do was keep alert, maybe catch a fleeting glimpse of green and yellow, and come back to tell him about it. If the bird hadn't been missing long, he couldn't have gotten very far.

This wasn't the first time I had searched for a lost bird. A few years earlier a resident on my route had lost a cockatiel. She put a big sign in her front yard and tacked flyers to telephone poles offering a reward to anyone who spotted it. About two weeks later, on a rainy, gloomy day, I saw the bird on the ground between two houses. The poor thing looked exhausted and bedraggled. It wouldn't last long with all the cats roaming the neighborhood.

I drove back to the house to tell her where I had seen the bird. She came running, barely believing the cockatiel could still be outside and alive. It was, and after a few days of loving attention, it made a full recovery. The signs came down a day later, and I never heard a word about the reward, but at least the bird had survived its little adventure.

I looked back at Mr. Harris. In his prime he had been a big fellow, but the years had withered him down to a mere shadow of his youth. He shuffled along slowly with his hands in his pockets, eyes aloft.

At the corner I crossed the street to work back up the other side. With the old man's pace, I would get to his house at the far end of the block long before he did. He startled me with another loud whistle as I drew up directly across the street from him. When I looked over, I realized he was too caught up in the search to be aware of my presence.

I continued looking for the bird. I had the idea that the little creature probably couldn't fly up into the tallest trees, so I narrowed my search to hedges and bushes. It would be nice to help the old man if I could; besides, I was early and in no hurry.

I've always liked older people. Perhaps it's because I'm interested in history, so I enjoy listening to their stories. And I always remember something my father told me years ago. We were driving in his car when an old man suddenly turned in front of us without using his turn signal. My father was known for his short temper.

"Doesn't that make you angry?" I asked, waiting for him to hit the horn.

He looked at me calmly and replied, "You have to cut the old folks some slack. We'll all be old some day, you know, and it can't be easy."

Walking into Mr. Harris's yard, I saw his wife sweeping off the front steps. We exchanged greetings as I handed her their mail. Pointing back over my shoulder, I said, "I saw your husband down the block. I'm sorry to hear your bird got away."

A bittersweet smile spread across her face as she looked down the street at her husband. "We haven't had that bird for twenty-five years," she said softly.

I suppose I should have seen that coming. It certainly explained some of the odd conversations we had had. But I was surprised, and saddened a little as well.

"It's been happening like this for the last few years," she explained. "The first warm day of the year, when the breeze blows just so, often triggers a memory for him of when we had a parakeet, and it did escape for a few hours."

I didn't know what to say. I just stared down the block at the frail old man. With a back bowed under the weight of his years, and hands crammed deep in his pockets, the old eyes still searched the treetops with an earnest intensity.

"But it's okay," she said. "At least he's getting some exercise." I turned to meet her friendly smile, and she added, "Isn't it a splendid day?"

Office Hours

When Danny decides to grace us with a song, the entire station stops to listen. Not because he's a great singer, which he isn't, but because it's just so startling to hear a middle-aged man suddenly break out in song on the workroom floor. He ignores our groans and catcalls. If he starts in a key that's too high, he stops, holds his hands up, and shouts, "Wait! Wait! Let me start over." Then, amid jeers and laughter, Danny begins again. Soon he's ripping headlong through "New York, New York," "Back in the USSR," or "All Shook Up." He may not be Frank, or Paul, or Elvis, but he knows all the words to all the verses, and he isn't afraid to belt them out.

Adding to the fun is our unspoken anticipation. We peek down Danny's way to see if he's about to let loose. He doesn't take requests, and if we ask him to sing he refuses, but when he finally gets going, we yell out guesses as to the original artist and when the song was recorded. We grimace when Danny strains to reach the high notes and laugh out loud at his hip-swaying, finger-snapping style.

≡✉≡

DANNY'S A CAPELLA RENDITIONS are a welcome diversion
on Saturday mornings after a long week of work. The only
days that all letter carriers have off together are Sundays and
holidays, so our Saturdays are like everyone else's Fridays, and
they tend to be a little more festive. If someone wants to treat
the station to rolls or cake for a birthday or anniversary, they
do it on Saturday. With all the miles we walk each day, letter
carriers are not timid about early morning calories.

A few years ago I worked with Carla, a letter carrier who
owned a lakeshore cabin a couple hours north of Minneapolis.
During summer months she often wanted to spend weekends
with her family at the lake, but her rotating schedule gave her a
Saturday off only once every six weeks. So she devised her own
little escape plan. After sending her husband and two children
ahead to the cabin on Friday night, she came to work on Saturday morning with a large bag of fast-food breakfast burgers.
She opened the bag and then set about sorting mail. Because
we start our workday so early, people often skip breakfast for
an extra snooze on the alarm. It didn't take long for curious letter carriers to investigate the mouth-watering aromas.

"What's in the bag, Carla? Have any extras?"

"Take a block off me and you can have one."

By nine o'clock she had given away most of her route, and
by noon she was on the beach at the cabin with her family. Of
course, the supervisors sanctioned none of this, but it was easy
for fifteen or twenty letter carriers to absorb an extra block
each, especially when the price was so right.

≡✉≡

ONE SUMMER, word got around our post office that a young
woman living nearby liked to sunbathe topless in her yard.
Like most other people, she had weekends off, so Saturday was
a big tanning day for her. To get the best angle on the sun's
rays, she lay out in her side yard, almost in the path of her letter carrier. Not too many Saturdays went by before our supervisor addressed us on the PA system. "Listen up, everyone. We
just received a complaint call. Last Saturday nine postal jeeps
were spotted driving past a certain nearby house. That was
nine jeeps before 12:00 noon." He couldn't help laughing along
with the rest of us. "Just knock it off," he concluded.

≡✉≡

IT'S A CHALLENGING JOB, with physical demands and the ever-
present knowledge that all that mail has to be delivered every
day regardless of the weather. A certain determined individu-
alism is necessary for survival. People not physically up to
the task don't last very long. Several years ago, during a short
stretch of time, five new letter carriers began working in our
station. Before their ninety-day probations were completed,
two had been let go for not moving fast enough on the street
and the other three had quit. I once saw a new substitute carrier standing in the middle of the workroom floor at the end of
a long day, his face flushed red from exertion. He leaned forward to ease the ache in his back, his jacket open and his head
and shoulders slouched in defeat. "I don't know how you folks
do this for thirty years," he lamented. "I've been here thirty

days, and I'm done." He walked out the door, and we never saw him again.

I work with a fellow who has two brothers delivering mail, and another's father is a retired carrier. The mother of yet another co-worker runs sorting machines downtown. There are many more. In a way, I've felt like an outsider my entire career because, as far as I know, no one else in my family has ever worked for the United States Postal Service.

The family connection seems to foster loyalty to the job. The uniform might play a small part in it, but more significant are the stories handed down by family members: tales of freak storms, crazy dogs, and the countless miles walked in a career. These carriers with a family history in the post office are the ones who keep telephone books handy to seek out correct addresses for misaddressed envelopes. They're the ones who, after work and on their own time, bring stamps out to their elderly patrons or mail packages for them at the holidays.

On our station wall is a black-and-white photograph of the letter carriers, clerks, and supervisors working out of our station half a century ago. In the back row is a smirking young man with wavy black hair at the beginning of his career. When I met Bob at the beginning of my own career, he was still smirking, but his hair had turned gray; he was a soon-to-be retired grandfather. More than thirty years older than I, he could still whip me on the tennis courts. He had the physical stamina and competitive spirit that is needed to wrestle a walking route under control every day, year after year.

The job of delivering mail hasn't changed much from the

time of Bob's career to mine, but a couple of facts can be extrapolated from that old photograph. For one thing, there were more carriers in the station then, which means there were more routes, which in turn suggests that the routes were shorter than they are today.

The gray steel shelving in the photo is still in use today, and it's identical to the shelving found in post offices across the country. I could transfer to Florida or Alaska, and I would be right at home in the workroom. These massive steel shelves are known as "cases." Each unit has five tiers of pigeonholes, with one slot for each address; three units per route are arranged in a U-shape, allowing the carrier to stand in the center and have access to all the slots. "Casing mail" is the term we use for sorting into these shelves.

Most of today's mail is transported by air. All the commercial airlines carry mail, even on Sundays. That's the reason that we handle nearly twice as much mail on Mondays. Throw in a Monday holiday, and Tuesday mornings greet us with three days' worth of mail.

Carriers arrive for work even earlier than usual the day after a holiday. Dispatches of mail have been arriving at the station since the middle of the night. Many times, one or two dispatches will have arrived during the holiday. Mail handlers and clerks disperse the mail to the routes. The familiar white USPS tubs filled with "flats"—magazines and catalogs—as well as plastic trays of letters are stacked hip-high around the cases.

We dig into it, and a silence borne of concentration and anxiety settles over the workroom floor. The Postal Service has established minimum standards for casing mail, but working four or even five times standard on heavy days can feel like a losing battle. Packages pile up, and mail is stacked everywhere. The dock doors bang open and groans erupt: more incoming mail.

Carriers rock from foot to foot while shoving mail into cases. Hunched shoulders and wired-tight postures reflect the tension. A morning radio talk show drones in the background, while some carriers isolate themselves in their own headphones. Occasionally, a stack of tubs tumbles over, spilling flats across the floor. The nearest carriers turn to look to make sure the avalanche hit no one, and then quickly resume the task of casing. Everyone is aware of the morning ticking away. In our station, we have an unwritten rule that no one should mention the time out loud, as that only intensifies the anxiety. And all this mail still has to be delivered today.

Eventually, the first carriers begin leaving for the street, and an earnest panic sets in on those still casing. There's the fear of not being able to get the job done, of having to call in to the supervisor to send help out to finish the route. Worst of all is the possibility of having to find addresses in the dark. At some point in their careers, all letter carriers have had the experience of stumbling around in the dark trying to read addresses by streetlight, especially during the early winter evenings.

If this sounds like a nightmare, it is. Our morning routine is the backdrop for many carriers' bad dreams. After hearing my descriptions of these early morning trials, my wife began having sympathetic nightmares for me. She has the details down, too. In her dream, which varies little from the ones my friends at work have described, she tries frantically to put letters in the case, but she can't fit them in the slot. She discards letters and grabs new ones, while carriers around her leave for the street. Eventually, she's the only one left, and she still hasn't put a single letter in the case. In another version she pulls up to a corner with a jeep full of mail. Opening the back door, she finds trays of mail stacked to the roof. She doesn't know where to begin, and it's getting dark out. (In letter-carrier nightmares, it's always getting dark out.) Frantically running up to houses, she finds that none of the addresses match those on the mail. She finally wakes herself up with her fitful tossing and turning.

When casing mail, we encounter a steady stream of undeliverable letters. These consist of misaddressed envelopes and mail to be forwarded or put on vacation hold. It might be mail with a good address but an unknown name, or a letter to someone who moved years ago. There are a number of specific reasons why a piece of mail may be undeliverable, but the stack of letters, bundled together, is known as "skulch." The regular carrier on the route is responsible for sorting through this stack every day, directing the individual pieces to the proper channels for processing.

Skulch is a term that is unique to the post office. You won't find it in the dictionary, but ask any letter carrier about skulch and you'll get a response. I've wondered about the word for years; where did it come from, and who coined it? Bob, the retired letter carrier, once told me the term was in common use fifty years ago, and had been around for decades before that.

It may be a funny sounding word, but skulch is a term we use every day in the post office, and it describes an important facet of a letter carrier's job. Ask your carrier about skulch sometime. The fact that you even know the word will probably get a grin out of him, unless he's just returned from vacation, in which case he probably has several bundles of it back at the station demanding his attention.

Most post offices have one-way mirrors. These aren't for spying on customers. Around the perimeter of the workroom is a hidden walkway, or crawlspace. Every ten or twelve feet, a one-way piece of glass is situated to give the observer, often a postal inspector, an unobstructed view of letter carriers working at their cases. To my knowledge, these spy ports are seldom used, although I have no way of knowing that. They're intended for a time when a station receives complaints regarding stolen mail, or pilfered letters like birthday cards, that may contain cash. An inspector can watch a suspected carrier casing mail to see if anything goes into a pocket.

I've heard of letter carriers getting fired for stealing, and these one-way mirrors probably play a role in proving guilt. But I've never worked with a letter carrier who exhibited anything less than complete respect for the mail. Besides, our jobs, benefits, and pensions are too important to risk. That's why a dollar bill lying on the workroom floor will still be there days later. No one wants to be seen putting cash in his or her pocket. You never know who may be watching.

The number of college-educated letter carriers I work with is amazing. Steve has a degree in English literature, while

Tim was an economics major and earned a master's degree in philosophy. Jeff taught elementary school his first year out of college. After realizing that teaching wasn't the career for him, he followed his father into the letter-carrying profession.

"I had no intention of staying here for thirty years," Jeff confided one morning as we cased mail, our easy rhythm of throwing letters providing Jeff a platform for storytelling. "I'd grown up listening to my dad's horror stories about the job. He grumbled all the time about working Saturdays, and he hated getting up so early. Hell, I hate it, too," he added with a self-mocking shake of the head. "My dad came home every night stiff and sore from trudging through the snow. I should have known better. Besides, I really didn't want to work with my dad, or hang around with his old work buddies. I was still young, I had a college education, and I thought I should be doing more."

I waited for him to continue, and when he didn't, I had to prod him. "But here you are. What made you decide to stay?"

"I don't think I ever consciously made that decision," Jeff said. "It was meant to be a temporary stopover, a way to make an income until I figured out what I wanted to do. There were college loans to pay. I needed a job."

That made sense. I know many carriers who started out planning to stay only a couple of years. Before long, they got enough seniority to bid on their own route and developed a comfortable routine. Life itself has a way of making some of these decisions for us. There's marriage, and children. Soon you can't afford to try something different, or you simply lose your nerve.

"I had a good friend back in those days," he continued. "We'd been roommates in college. We talked about my dilemma for hours on end. He helped me realize that I wasn't really wasting my college education. A good education is never wasted, because it becomes a part of who you are. But even more important, I came to understand that blue-collar work` could be as satisfying as any job. It's what you bring to it, and the effort you put out, that's important."

Before I could comment, Jeff added, "It's like my friend explained to me one time; if you're going to be a mailman, then be the best damn mailman you can be."

After thinking about that for a minute, I asked, "Where's your friend now? He seems like a pretty wise fellow—what does he think of your thirty-year career?"

"He passed away several years ago," Jeff replied. "It was really hard. You know how it is; he was young, it was unexpected, and he left behind a wife and son."

"I'm really sorry," I said.

"Well, I kept in touch with his family, you know, in case I could do something for them. He'd been such an important friend to me. In a way, I hoped that maybe I could honor his friendship by helping his family."

"And how did that go?" I asked.

A wry grin appeared on Jeff's face. Then he chuckled. "I watched his son grow up. Like I said, I dropped in on them from time to time. We'd play some catch in the yard, or just sit around talking. About the time he entered high school, I noticed that he began losing direction in his life, and I thought,

'Okay, this is where I can do something to repay my friend's kindness.'"

I picked up another tub of flats, but Jeff's story had tweaked my interest. Replacing the bucket, I stepped over to his case, and asked, "So what did you do? Play one of those big-brother roles? Were you able to help him?"

He set a bundle of letters aside and looked at me. "You have to remember, I was trained as a teacher. You'd think I would know something about motivating a kid." He shook his head, laughing at the memory. "I had nothing. God, it was frustrating. It nagged at me constantly." He thrust his arms out. "Here was my chance to repay my old friend, and I had absolutely nothing. It seemed that whenever I spent time with the kid, he slid further away."

"I'm sure you did everything you could," I said.

Jeff hung his head. "He took up playing the guitar. Eventually, he dropped out of school. Don't get me wrong, he was a good kid. We had some great discussions. He just didn't have any direction. At least, not any direction that I could relate to."

"He probably just wasn't ready to hear you," I suggested. After a moment, I asked, "Whatever happened to him?"

Jeff picked up the stack of letters. He threw an embarrassed grin over his shoulder before turning away to resume casing. "I guess it all worked out in the end," he said. "No thanks to me. The kid started a little rock-and-roll band called Soul Asylum. Ever heard of them?"

Cowboy

There are dozens of wonderful dogs living on my route. Some of them bark like demons at everyone else but whimper and whine impatiently as I approach their yards. Lady, a big black lab, sits at the window each day waiting for my truck to pull up at the corner. Then she runs to get her owner to let her out so she can greet me at the gate. There's an old, gray-faced beagle that bays with delight when he sees me, and a miniature collie that dances in circles with excitement. On any given day, I probably meet and talk to more dogs than people.

I've heard all the jokes about the antagonistic relationship between letter carriers and dogs. In fact, I know two or three that would eat me if they got the chance. But by rattling a gate, or watching closely before entering their yard, I have avoided serious conflicts. Staying alert helps—a person down the block jingling car keys, sounding like the collar and tags of an attacking dog, will set off a surge of adrenaline.

At one house, a painted black-and-white sheet-metal placard is nailed to the wall next to the "NO SOLICITORS" sign.

Silhouetted in profile is a doberman pincher, and the words, "I can get to the gate in 1.3 seconds. Can you?"

Even the bad dogs, once they get used to seeing me every day, usually mellow out. The fact that I carry dog biscuits doesn't hurt, either. I dole out biscuits like protection money, a small fee to ensure safe passage.

For example, I've known a certain pit bull since he was a puppy. The first time I saw him chained next to the house, I decided I had better make friends before he grew up. After two years we're good pals, and he waits quietly every day for me to come around with his biscuit. One day his owner was in the yard, and I asked, "If your dog ever got loose, do you think he'd bite me?"

"Man, don't ever go near him," he replied with a sneer. "That dog even scares me most days."

"Oh, yeah? Watch this," I said, walking over to the dog straining at the end of his logging chain.

The owner protested, "Don't do that, man!"

I knelt beside the dog, and he shoved his big square head against my chest. I wrapped an arm around him and patted his thick shoulder. It was a silly thing to do, but the stunned look on the owner's face made it worthwhile.

When I got up, the man persisted, "You're lucky he didn't take your arm off. Nobody pets that dog!"

"Well, maybe you should," I replied. "I've been doing it for two years now. He likes it."

There was another dog on my route, a rottweiler, that really scared me. He was tied with a flimsy rope that stretched to within a few feet of the mailbox on the porch. I had talked to the owners about that, and they promised to shorten the rope, but it never happened. This dog had me completely intimidated. He was massive, and every day he let me know how much he hated me. He had a deep-throated, growling bark and a nasty habit of snarling and gnashing his teeth while lunging at me. My dog biscuit offerings were ignored; this maniac wanted fresh meat.

I watched the rope deteriorating in the elements, and I knew that it was only a matter of time before something bad happened. But as much as I dreaded delivering mail to their house, it was the attitude of the young men who lived there that really angered me. I got madder by the day. When one of the owners stood in the doorway, watching the dog bark and lunge at me, the sound of snapping teeth finally pushed me over the edge. I yelled, "If that dog ever gets loose and attacks me, I'll kill him."

The young man stepped outside, affecting a look of surprise. I threw his mail on the steps and said, "When that rope snaps and it comes down to him or me, believe me, buddy, I won't lose."

He snickered and opened the door to call to his roommate. "Hey, the mailman is going to kill our dog."

I was infuriated. The only thing I could do was get away from there. The problem resolved itself in a few weeks, however, when the police raided the house for drugs. I never saw the owners, or the dog, again.

BUT COWBOY WAS DIFFERENT. He was a big, mixed-breed dog with the dull yellow color of a lab and the longer, feathered fur of a retriever. In contrast with his lackluster yellow fur, he wore a bright red bandana tied around his collar. Cowboy didn't have a mean bone in his body. One of his best friends was a neighbor's old orange tabby cat that liked to snuggle up with him in the sun for a nap.

The house where Cowboy lived was set well back from the street. His owner was a handyman carpenter who had built a beautiful cedar fence around the yard to keep Cowboy at home. It probably wasn't necessary, however, as the few times I saw him out of the yard, Cowboy just sat near the gate watching the world go by. When he spotted me, he accompanied me around the block.

His doghouse was out back by the alley. When he heard me come through the gate, he tore around the corner of the house and across the front yard to greet me. If he didn't happen to hear me, I gave a short whistle just to watch him come running. I always took a minute to sit on the steps and scratch his ears.

Cowboy was one of those rare dogs whose expressions showed on his face. His mouth always seemed to turn up in a smile when I arrived; but then, I only saw him for these few brief moments each day, so maybe that was just the shape of his mouth. He used his whole body to wag his tail when greeting me.

Cowboy's living situation was unusual. His owners were divorced. The woman lived in the house, but I seldom saw her. The handyman husband kept an apartment nearby, but

I talked to him at the house all the time. He mowed the lawn
and did all the upkeep around the place. And, of course, he
built that beautiful fence. I commented one time on their living arrangements. His reply was simple and straightforward.

"I still love her," he said. "I guess we can't live together, but
I want her in my life. Besides, there's Cowboy to think about.
My apartment doesn't allow dogs, so I come over every day to
visit him."

Whenever we stood around talking, Cowboy would lie in
the grass nearby watching us. He looked like he thought it was
just the greatest thing in the world to be hanging around with
his two best buddies.

Then, one hot summer day, they met me at the gate. "My
wife passed away last night in her sleep," the handyman said,
choking on the words.

I was stunned. "I didn't even know she was sick," I stammered. But it explained why he was always working around the
house, and why I rarely saw her.

They held the funeral service the next Saturday at a neighborhood church. Family and friends from all over the country
attended. By noon, the street in front of Cowboy's house was
lined with cars. The yard was full of well-dressed people, and
friends of the family had two long tables of food set up along
the fence.

The handyman met me at the gate when I came by on my
rounds. I had never seen him in a suit before, but even the finest clothes couldn't hide his sorrow. I offered my condolences.
We searched for things to say, commenting on the large turn-

out of people and how the weather was perfect for an outdoor gathering.

He said, "Her mail is being forwarded out west to her sister's house."

"Yeah, I know." I had processed the change of address forms that morning.

"They're going to sell the house."

"What about Cowboy?" I asked.

"He's going out west, too. I'm driving him out to Montana myself."

We stood for a moment in awkward silence while I searched for words of comfort. The voices of the guests became a soft drone in the background. He must have thought I was still worrying about Cowboy, because he said, "He'll be living out in the country, and he'll have lots of room to run. I'll stay with him for a while to make sure he's okay."

I nodded. Looking around the yard, I saw women in black dresses and high heels, men in sport coats and western boots, but no dog. "Where is Cowboy?" I asked.

"I think he finally figured out what happened," he said. "He's taking it pretty hard. Maybe he's worried about what will happen now." Looking around the yard, he added, "I suppose he's sulking out back in his doghouse."

I stalled for a few moments, scanning the crowd for a colorful bandana. It seemed unlikely that Cowboy was fretting over his future, but I found myself worrying for him. It didn't seem right to just walk away. Finally, on a whim, I asked, "Do you mind if I go in and say good-bye to him?"

"That would be wonderful," he said, smiling and opening the gate for me. "I'm sure he'd like that."

I began the long walk across the front yard to the house. Guests turned to look at me, eyeing my uniform and satchel full of mail. Near the steps a woman in a long black dress approached. The family resemblance was obvious.

"If you have anything for my sister, I can take it," she said. "I'm having her mail forwarded to me."

"I know. I already sent it on." Looking toward the side of the house, I added, "Actually, I was hoping to see Cowboy. We've been good friends, and I wanted to say good-bye."

She looked around. "I haven't seen him lately. Maybe he's inside."

"He might be out back," I said, giving my short whistle. From the reactions of people standing near the side of the house, I knew I was right. Faces turned to watch as the big dog tore around the house, clumps of sod flying when he made the turn. He almost knocked me down.

We took up our customary seats on the front steps. I had never seen him so animated, and I laughed when he licked my chin. He snuggled so close he almost climbed inside my satchel.

"I know, I know, Cowboy. I'm going to miss you, too." When I scratched his ears, it seemed as if the corners of his mouth turned up again. Sitting tight against him, I could feel the big dog calming down. He leaned over and licked my face again, and I had to wipe my chin on my sleeve.

Someone muttered, "Look, the mailman is saying good-bye to Cowboy."

"You're going to have a real nice place to live," I told him. "I bet there will be lots of places to run and explore." I assured him that everything would be okay.

We sat together for several minutes until I became aware of the surrounding silence. When I looked up, the whole yard full of people was watching us.

Standing up, I leaned over to give him one last pat on the head. "You be a good dog, Cowboy. Everything's going to be just fine."

He made no attempt to follow when I walked away. Guests shuffled aside as I crossed the yard. Even the food servers stopped what they were doing to look at the big yellow dog. Many eyes were moist, and I saw a large man wearing a Stetson hat pull out his handkerchief.

At the gate, the handyman shook my hand. "Thanks," he said.

We turned to look at Cowboy still perched on the steps. The sister was petting him, and a few of the other guests began fussing over him, too. Cowboy enjoyed the attention, his tongue lolling out of his mouth in time to his panting.

Setting off on my route again, I knew I was going to miss him. But I was glad I had said good-bye, if for no other reason than to see the smile return to Cowboy's face.

Delivering Reality

On a Saturday morning in one of my first months on my regular assignment, the accountables clerk handed me a registered letter. Generally speaking, the few pieces of registered mail I've handled contain coins or gems. This doesn't happen too often on a blue-collar, residential route like mine.

When a customer goes to the expense of registering a letter, the window clerk signs for it, enters it in a log book, gives the customer a receipt, and locks the piece of mail in the office safe. Later, when the truck driver arrives to take our outgoing mail downtown for processing, he signs for it. Most drivers carry a pouch to keep such an item safe until it's delivered to an accountables clerk downtown. Once again it's signed for. An individual accounts for every leg of the journey for a registered letter. Losing one can be grounds for dismissal.

Although they are rare, I have handled insured registered letters valued in the tens of thousands of dollars. In 1968, the Postal Service very quietly delivered the Hope Diamond, registered and insured for $1,000,000. If you're the type to

ponder the nature of reality, just join the Postal Service. Toss
in a registered letter, and it doesn't get any more real than that.
Like a mortgage payment, or the anxiety leading up to tax day,
the Postal Service is all about reality.

Letter carriers guard a piece of registered mail with assidu-
ous attention. I usually secure it in an inside pocket. Until it's
delivered and signed for by the customer, or safely returned to
the accountables clerk, a registered letter is a nagging presence
in the back of a carrier's mind.

I could count on one hand the number of registered letters
I had handled in my short career, so I was startled on this
Saturday morning when the accountables clerk asked for my
signature. Even more surprising was the condition of the letter.
Smudged, dirty, dog-eared, it looked like a museum specimen.
We studied it together, calling other carriers to have a look.

The postage consisted of several colorful stamps from Vietnam. Near them was a receiving postmark in San Francisco.
We looked at each other in wonder when my finger underlined
the receiving date: 1976. The letter had arrived in the United
States at least fourteen years earlier. The original address was
faded and crossed out, but we deciphered a Vietnamese name
(or at least an Asian name) and *General Delivery* in San Francisco. None of us had ever seen a registered letter addressed to
General Delivery.

Below that, someone had penciled in another address in
San Francisco, but that one was also crossed out. Various offi-
cial stamps blotted the envelope: NO SUCH ADDRESS, or MOVED,
LEFT NO FORWARDING. Without a return address to work with,

carriers in California had kept the letter alive. Four or five addresses had been hand printed, with notes added, such as, "Try here," or "Please forward to . . ."

Each one was scratched out.

We followed the trail of addresses around northern California. Then, in the lower right-hand corner, were the words, "Moved to Oregon in 1983." An arrow pointed to the flip side of the envelope. On the back we found an address for a church in Portland. More hand-written addresses, more postmarks: 1984, 1985. The trail led to Seattle, and by 1987 the letter had meandered up to Missoula, Montana.

In the late 1980s, the letter stopped twice in Bismarck, North Dakota. Then it was off to Minot. At that point, in smudged black ink, the words FORWARDING ORDER EXPIRED were stamped across the address. A heavy black finger of ink pointed out that the letter should be returned to the sender. Of course, there was no return address, and once again, in the spirit of getting the mail delivered, a letter carrier in Minot, North Dakota, had written in the address of a small house on my route in South Minneapolis.

I stared at the address. There was no mistake; the numerals were printed clearly. Even the zip code was correct. I shook my head in bewilderment. While the accountables clerk explained to the other carriers what we were looking at, I turned the envelope over and looked at the name again. Attempting to sound out the letters, I decided it had the ring of a feminine name. The printing, old and faded as it was, looked masculine.

A love letter?

The only address not crossed out was the one on my route. We speculated about where the letter had lain for months or years between attempted deliveries. The clerk asked, "Does that name look familiar?"

I pictured the house on my route. Even though I had been on this assignment only a short time, I knew many of the names of the residents. A young couple lived in that particular house, a young couple with an infant child and a common, everyday name like Thompson, or Johnson—nothing even close to the exotic name on the envelope.

I shook my head, but the significance of what I held in my hands began to dawn on me. For fourteen years, letter carriers had found ways to push this letter toward a destination. Machines process undeliverable mail, but if the computer doesn't have a forwarding address on file, the letter is returned to the carrier to begin the journey back to the sender. Unlike computerized machines, however, letter carriers wouldn't let this one die. They talked to neighbors and rummaged through old records to keep it alive.

In handwriting sometimes clear and purposeful, other times scrawled in pencil or bright red ink, they had passed it along. One address was circled several times in dark blue ink to make it stand out from the others, as if the carrier had been sure this would be the final destination. Ultimately, that one was crossed out too, and now it sat in my hands.

"I've never seen this name before," I said to the clerk. "And I know who lives at this address."

The clerk asked carriers on routes near mine to see if they recognized the name. Perhaps a number in the address had been accidentally transposed. Again, I looked at the original postmark. The stamps had been canceled in Saigon. Hadn't Saigon fallen in 1975? Wasn't that Ho Chi Minh City now? I was on my first route, and I suddenly felt a responsibility of historic proportions on my shoulders. *Reality* rested in my fingertips.

"It's Saturday," the clerk stated flatly, handing me the clipboard to sign for the letter. "Someone will probably be home. If they've never heard of this person, bring it back and we'll kill it."

His words stunned me. To "kill it" simply meant we would endorse it as attempted delivery. Under normal circumstances it would then be returned to the sender. In this case, however, it would go to the dead letter office. We would, literally, kill it.

My mind was in a fog as I cased mail for the rest of the route. The significance of 1975 in Saigon was not lost on me. I remembered the news film of the last helicopters yanking the final evacuees from the U.S. embassy before the Viet Cong overran the city. The mysterious purpose of the letter became a distraction, its contents haunting my thoughts far more than the most valuable registered letter I had ever carried. Also nagging at me was the diligence of all those carriers, through all the years, working to get this letter delivered. Now that responsibility had somehow fallen to me.

I pictured a gray-haired letter carrier, hunched over the envelope, black-rimmed reading glasses slipping down his nose

as he carefully penciled in another address. Or maybe a young
carrier new to her route had played at detective and passed
on her hunch about a destination. Perhaps a Vietnam vet had
handled it.

The sun was bright and warm on that Saturday morning.
We got our customary safety talk from the supervisor advising
us to be vigilant for loose dogs, more common on Saturdays.
But dogs were the last things on my mind. I loaded out my
mail, started up the jeep, and tried to focus on the job at hand.
I walked off the first couple of blocks, but couldn't find my
stride. That letter was eating at me. It seemed I had been given
a test, and I felt unworthy. All those other carriers had found
ways to keep this letter alive. I feared their efforts would be
wasted. Would it all end here today, with me?

I became convinced that it was a love letter, perhaps from
a boyfriend or husband. The person the envelope was addressed to must have escaped from Saigon before the end of
the war. My only hope was that somehow the young couple on
my route would have knowledge of this person. It was a long
shot, but then why had this particular address been so clearly
penciled in? After all these years, and all those miles, it seemed
heartless to just bring the letter back to be killed, even if these
patrons couldn't solve the puzzle.

The distraction, the mystery, finally got the best of me. The
house was near the end of the route, but I couldn't wait any
longer. My heart racing with anticipation, I ripped off my mail
satchel, dug out the letter that by now seemed to weigh a ton,
and took off in the jeep.

As I pulled up to the house I was struck by the absurdity of it all. This young couple had been mere children when the letter was mailed. What could they possibly know? Braced for disappointment, I pushed the doorbell, then again studied the foreign stamps and the word "SAIGON" clearly stamped across them.

The door opened and I looked up to see the young man of the house, smiling pleasantly and holding a baby in his arms. I stepped forward, showing him the envelope, unsure how to begin.

"Do you know anyone with a name like this?" I blurted. Because the writing was so faded and lost among all the addresses, I held my index finger below the name. "I have to ask," I continued, choking off a self-conscious chuckle, "because it's a registered letter, and someone put your address on it."

The man leaned forward to squint at the name. I found myself squeezing the paper as if he might try to steal it away from me. He stepped back. "Just a minute," he said, and turned to call to his wife.

"Well, this is just ridiculous," I thought. "You can't decide for yourself whether you've seen a foreign name like this before?"

When his wife came to the door, he nodded at the envelope still clutched firmly in my fingers. "You better take a look at this," he said.

I held it up for her, and watched her eyes slide from the name to the stamps in the corner. "Oh, my God," she muttered. As she stepped back, the envelope slid from my fingers into her hand. An elderly Asian woman stood behind her. Dressed in a floor-length skirt, with a colorful scarf around her head, she moved forward as the younger woman made room for her.

With exaggerated jabs of her finger, the wife pointed at the name on the envelope. A wail exploded from the old woman. She grabbed the letter and clutched it to her breast with both hands. She whirled in circles, her long skirt trailing out, and from her lips erupted an otherworldly keening. On and on she twirled, tears flying.

The young woman looked at me with an expression of utter joy, tears streaming down her face. The baby fidgeted, startled by the sudden racket, and looked at his father's tear-filled eyes. The husband joined me out on the front steps. He explained that their church had taken this woman in, and he and his wife had offered to have her stay for a while with them. The woman's husband had died in the war. The letter was from her son. They had been separated at the end of the war. Over the years, she had passed through several churches and social service organizations, never bothering to change her address because she never received any mail—until now. A few years earlier she learned that her son had survived in various refugee camps, but the letter I delivered was the first and only physical proof she had of his existence.

Behind us, the wailing subsided to sobs and moans. The woman had dropped to her knees. I glimpsed the young wife bending over her, hands bracing the shoulders of the tiny Vietnamese lady. The old face was contorted in furrows of anguish and joy.

The young man signed for the letter, effectively clearing

me of responsibility. After all the determination and persever-
ance of those letter carriers, I got to be the one to witness the
results. Now I understood why they had taken the time, and as
I walked back to my jeep, I wiped the reality of it off my cheeks.

Let Me See You

I worried about Evelyn when I noticed all the cars parked in front of her house and folks going up to her doorstep. I knew she was quite old, but I could only guess at her age. Once she told me that her husband had passed away twenty years earlier, and he had been retired for ten years before that, so she had to be in her mid-nineties.

Small, trim, and wiry, Evelyn had lived alone all the years I had known her. She was somewhat hard of hearing, but we had several chats over the years. A sense of humor twinkled in her eyes. Because she lived alone and didn't get out by herself, I insisted that I should see her every day. She didn't have to come to the door, but I wanted to see her nonetheless. Most days she was sitting in an overstuffed easy chair by her living room window watching the daily soaps. A simple wave was all I needed to know that she was all right.

At any given time I usually have an arrangement like this with one or two shut-ins on my route. Receiving a piece of mail or a phone call from a friend or relative might be the highlight of someone's day, and I might be his or her sole daily contact with the outside world. So waving to me isn't an inconvenience for them, and it may very well make them feel a little safer and not quite so alone.

=✉=

I STARTED DOING THIS early on, after an incident involving another elderly woman. Living on a fixed income, she was slowly losing the battle of maintaining her house. Given her age, she could offer only token efforts at the yard work. A few perennials adorned the edges of her front steps, but the lawn had been taken over by weeds and large bare spots. One summer day I found her sitting upright on the ground in her front yard, with her legs splayed out in front and her nylon stockings rolled down just above her ankles. Using a scissor-style grass clipper, she was cutting the grass as far around her as she could reach. Then she ponderously rocked her heavy frame over a few feet to begin on a new swatch.

She was a cantankerous old lady. The neighbors told me she wouldn't talk to anyone, and she was known to yell at children if they strayed off the city sidewalk into her yard. Approaching her one day as she worked the grass clipper, I offered to help start her lawn mower. She brushed me aside with a wave of her hand. I found out later she had sold the lawn mower to help pay her utility bills. All summer long her windows were wide open, emitting the sounds of a local news station on an AM radio.

For several days in a row I came by with her mail and heard the radio inside. As it happened, I usually arrived on her block around lunchtime. She had a mail slot that went directly into the house, so I didn't see the mail accumulating. It never occurred to me that anything was wrong. I figured she was eating lunch, or perhaps taking a nap. Then one day the neighbor told me what happened. After trying to sleep with his windows open, and hearing that darn radio all night long, he had finally gone over to ask her to turn it off. When she didn't come to the door, he called the police. They found her on the kitchen floor. She had been dead for a week.

I felt bad about it for a long time. It wasn't as though we were friends; she hadn't wanted that. But the thought of her dying alone, and lying there for so long, just wasn't right. After that, I decided to be more vigilant for the welfare of my older patrons.

BUT THEN THERE WAS the time my vigilance backfired. A lifelong bachelor once lived on my route. With curly white hair hanging over his ears and a long, thick, gray beard, he could have been an extra in a Civil War documentary. Tall and lean, with a wrinkled, weathered face, he was an eccentric character disguising himself as an intellectual. He didn't have a garage, so he parked his old Cadillac in the yard beside his house. The interior of the car was piled high with papers and junk, leaving just enough room for a driver to squeeze in behind the wheel. His house was the same way. On one of the rare times I peeked inside, I saw books, magazines, and newspapers stacked hip-high everywhere. Narrow passageways allowed navigation from room to room.

I saw the old guy often. Sometimes in the winter he sat in the old Cadillac working a crossword puzzle. The car would be idling, heater on high, the window open halfway. He always wore a distinctive white fur hat in cold weather. He couldn't have known—or cared about—what his neighbors had to say about his lifestyle.

He was very aware, however, of the schedule for delivery of his social security and retirement checks. He often met me in the yard on those days, wearing no coat or jacket; the familiar fur hat was always perched high on his head. So I thought it odd one spring day when he didn't show up to take his government check from me. The Cadillac was parked in its usual position. I considered knocking on his door, but he was a cranky, independent sort, and I didn't want to invade his space.

The next day, though, when I added his retirement pension check to the social security check in the mailbox, I did knock. No answer. A neighbor had once mentioned that they belonged to the same VFW post. He had seen the old bachelor having a beer there from time to time. I walked over to this neighbor's house and inquired after my lost patron.

"Haven't seen him," the man replied. "That piece-of-crap car hasn't moved in days, either."

I explained that his neighbor hadn't picked up his checks. "Do you know his phone number?"

He laughed. "The old coot didn't pay his phone bill, so they disconnected him. He hasn't had a phone in years. Hell, who'd ever want to call him, anyway?"

This sudden absence nagged at me, though. I swung by

at the end of the day to find the checks still there. I returned to my station and related my concerns to the supervisor. He immediately called the local police precinct. The authorities assured us we had done the right thing. They dispatched a squad car and I rushed back out to the house.

When I arrived, two officers made quick work of breaking in the front door. I waited as they entered, watching them file through the cluttered passageways. Finally, one of them emerged from the shattered doorway.

"He's not in there," he said. "Of course, I suppose he could be hidden somewhere in all that junk," he added with a snicker.

For several days thereafter I noted the deserted car, the plywood barricade the city had screwed on over the broken front door, and the mail filling up the mailbox. Then one morning his neighbor from the VFW met me. "Well," he began, an I-told-you-so smirk playing across his face, "the old geezer finally came home." He nodded up the street toward the old bachelor's house. Chuckling now, he told me, "One of his World War II buddies came to town, and they went off on a week-long bender. All the way down to Iowa and back."

After my initial sigh of relief, I had to laugh at the image of the old warrior carousing around the countryside with an old comrade-in-arms. I was still grinning as I approached the plywood doorway. The old man came stalking around the back corner of the house, and his look wiped the grin off my face.

In a voice way too loud for the short distance between us, he bellowed, "You know some son-a-bitch called the cops on me?

They broke my damn door down." His language startled me, and as I met his glance head on, the scales in my mind tipped from eccentric intellectual to complete lunatic. Spittle clung to his beard and red veins glowed in his eyes. "If I ever find out who did it, I'll rip the prying nose right off their face."

I feigned ignorance, and since then, I've fine-tuned my vigilance, understanding that each situation is unique.

=✉=

THE WAVING ARRANGEMENT that Evelyn and I used had served us well for years. I had never seen so many cars parked in front of her house, though, and as I approached I vividly recalled seeing her the day before. She had held her head canted to one side to better hear the television set, giving me her bright-eyed smile and a quick wave.

When I climbed the front steps, the door opened and a well-dressed young man met me. "Hi," he said, smiling. I dared to hope that everything was okay inside.

In an effort to confirm it, I asked, "Is Evelyn home? I have some mail for her."

"She's right here," he replied. Reaching out his hand, he introduced himself as her grandson. Behind him, I could see Evelyn talking to a room full of relatives.

"Grandma?" he called in a voice loud enough to be heard over the din in the room. To me, he said, "It's her birthday. Ninety-nine years old today."

Evelyn scurried over to the door. Her smile was wonderful to behold.

"Happy birthday," I offered, at a loss for anything better to say in front of a room full of strangers. Then, overcome with relief and the obvious pleasure in her smile at seeing me, I wrapped an arm around her frail shoulder and gave her a hug.

"Oh," she tittered, drawing back when I released her. "Is that all I get? A hug? You know, it isn't every day a girl turns ninety-nine."

Amid laughter from her gathered family, I planted a big kiss on her cheek. "Happy birthday, Evelyn!"

On her one-hundredth birthday we repeated the ritual, and again for her one hundred and first. After that, she moved into an assisted-living housing complex, and the married grandson took over the house.

It's wonderful to watch new life being restored to the neighborhood. After all, it's the younger generation that has the energy to update and maintain the old houses. Now great-grandchildren play where Evelyn once sat watching for my arrival. And I can see her twinkling eyes in theirs.

My Brother's Brother

For a short time a young mother, with her son and daughter, rented the first floor of a two-story duplex on my route. I didn't get to know them all that well because they moved on again in just a little more than a year. From change-of-address labels I knew they arrived in Minneapolis from the Red Lake Ojibwe Reservation in northern Minnesota, and they returned to the reservation when they left.

The six-year-old boy caught the school bus on the corner where I parked when delivering mail on their block. His thick black hair sprouted out in wild tufts, and he lugged a Winnie-the-Pooh backpack. His older sister, perhaps ten or eleven years old, accompanied him to the corner to catch the bus.

When we spoke, he always referred to me as "Sir," or "Mister." A couple of times I was startled, turning from putting mail in a box, to find him, watching me in silence. He had an odd way of staring off to the side when we talked. Sometimes his expression became so serious that it looked like his eyes didn't quite line up, as if he were studying something no one else could see.

Because he was so young his vocabulary was limited, but he spoke with that intriguing, musical Ojibwe lilt. He had a peculiar way of stringing words together, or maybe it was simply his delivery, that reminded me of an old man.

One day, he told me about a dog his family had once owned. When he said the dog's name was Blackie, I thought of a black lab, or some big, mixed-breed animal, until he informed me that the dog was actually yellow.

"Just his name was Blackie. He was a *good* dog," he said. "We played together in the woods near our house. I could go there only if Blackie came with me. He was a *good* dog," he repeated several times, shaking his head.

"What happened to him?" I asked.

"My uncle shot him," the boy replied. "But he was a *good* dog."

Sometime later, I learned from his sister that Blackie had been very old, and his uncle had put him down when he became sick.

The strangest conversation we had, however, occurred one morning when I encountered them waiting for the bus on the corner. Getting out of my jeep, I asked them how school was going. We stood there talking, the little boy describing a pet turtle he kept at school. Then the weirdest thing happened. I never saw the boy look up, but all of a sudden, midway through his description, he stopped and pointed at the sky. Then he slowly tipped his head back and searched the sky above us.

"Sis!" he exclaimed. "An eagle! We have to go home and do the tobacco."

His sister put an arm around his shoulder, explaining that it would be okay to wait until after school for the tobacco. She used an Ojibwe expression for the ritual, which I didn't understand. Because of the way the boy pointed at the sky before even looking up, I was a little suspicious of a practical joke. When I finally snuck a quick peek overhead, however, I was shocked to see a mature bald eagle gliding in lazy circles just fifty feet above the intersection.

I've seen many eagles in northern Minnesota, or along the Mississippi River, but never over a residential section of South Minneapolis. And the fact that the bird flew so low was a little unnerving. The strangest part was that he looked down at us. He was probably just wary of our presence, but I would have sworn he looked right at the little boy.

We watched the eagle for several moments before I asked the girl what her brother meant by "doing the tobacco." It took a while for her to respond. She was thinking, pursing her lips, and I wasn't sure if she didn't want to say, or didn't know how to say it. Finally, she told me they burn an offering of tobacco to honor the eagle's spirit.

I asked her why they honor the eagle. Even though she seemed uncomfortable talking about it, in the end I guess she decided it was okay because I was a friend of her brother.

"The eagle is my brother's totem," she said.

I nodded, although I wasn't too sure what that meant. Then she added, "The eagle is my brother's brother."

There were several ways to consider that answer, but the bus came before I could ask any more questions. Within seconds the children were gone, and the rumble of the school bus faded away around the corner. Before heading off down the block to deliver mail, I took one last look above me, but the eagle had disappeared, too.

Pride and Prejudice

While casing mail one morning I came across a photo on a postcard that caught my attention. I have to admit that taking a peek at the picture side of postcards is a habit. It takes but a moment to look at the picture and move on. I know that other carriers do the same, because when a truly unique card comes along, we tend to share the picture with each other. Of course, after you look at postcards for a couple of decades, they begin to lose their novelty. After all, how many views of the Grand Canyon, or some nameless beach in the tropics, do you want to see? But glancing at the photo side of cards has become a habit, if for no better reason than to break the monotony of casing mail.

Sometimes I'm amazed at the things people mail. I've delivered stamped coconuts from Hawaii, the address and message written in permanent black marker. One time I delivered a letter rolled up and sealed inside a plastic bottle. The address was written on a self-stick label, and the postage strip was wrapped around the neck of the bottle. I've listened to live pigeons in shipping crates with air holes, and handled cartons containing thousands of mealyworms for fishing. But perusing picture postcards as they come along is a daily affair. How some of them are allowed through the mail system is beyond me.

That was the nature of the postcard I came across this particular morning. The subject was a beach volleyball player in action. As she dove for a shot, she appeared to have played her well-endowed self right out of the top of her bikini. But the thing that really shocked me was that the card was addressed to a woman named Audrey, an elderly widow on my route.

Upon closer inspection, the handwriting looked familiar. Sure enough, the signature revealed that Audrey's retired next-door neighbor, Lorraine, had sent the card. Having raised their families next door to each other, they had been close friends for nearly fifty years. Both are widows, and I often see them with Lorraine's sister, Marilyn, driving off to garage sales or a day of shopping. They always honk and wave at me like a carload of teenage girls. Lorraine was on a short winter vacation in Arizona, thus the subject matter of the card.

I've always been a firm believer in the sanctity of the mail, and everyone's right to privacy. On the other hand, the message sides of postcards are right out there for anyone to see. This particular card had tweaked my curiosity. I knew Lorraine had a great sense of humor, but I couldn't imagine why she'd be sending such an explicit postcard to Audrey. So, even though I don't approve of reading someone else's mail . . .

Lorraine began with all the usual stuff, the sunny, warm weather in Arizona, and how nice it was to see flowers blooming in January. Then, right in the middle of the text, in capital letters, I read, "HI VINCE!" I was so surprised; it was like getting caught with my hand in the cookie jar. I actually looked behind me to see if anyone was watching. She went on, "I'm guessing that if you see this picture you'll be reading the card. I'll find out when I get home. Hope you have a nice day!" She even added one of those smiley faces.

I thought about playing dumb, but the next time I saw Lorraine I cracked up. "Aha!" she exclaimed, laughing at my inability to keep a straight face. "I knew you'd read that card."

IN THE AGING BLUE-COLLAR neighborhood where I deliver mail, I see many retired folks on a regular basis. Over the years I've developed some really close relationships. For instance, I've been invited to Lorraine's annual Christmas party for the last ten or fifteen years. The whole neighborhood, for blocks around, shows up. It's a huge open house with wonderful food. The party gives me the chance to talk with patrons for more than the couple of minutes I have when I see them on the route.

Another elderly woman on my route makes homemade caramel candies. She gives me a package of them each year, about fifty bite-sized, hand-formed squares meticulously wrapped in waxed paper, all tightly packed into a box originally used for chocolates.

This woman is also one of three retired ladies who scrounge the neighborhood together collecting aluminum cans. Wire baskets attached to their bicycles hold the bounty of their harvests. Dressed in sweat pants and old jackets and wearing rubber kitchen gloves, they'll even help each other climb into dumpsters in search of their quarry. When a chain slips off or a tire goes flat, they get their fingers right in there, smudging themselves up good with chain oil and grease. Sometimes they walk the neighborhood together, clearing cans, as well as other garbage, from the curbsides. When they've collected half a dozen large garbage bags of crushed cans, they haul them to the recycler, collect their pay, and use it to go out to lunch together.

I tease them regularly about their fashion statements, but they just laugh. Either they're beyond the age of caring what people think, or they just know better. I don't wave at them when they're on their bicycles anymore, though. Not since the time one of them took a hand off the handlebar to wave back and nearly crashed into a parked car.

It's a wonderful project on many levels. Not just the fact that they clean up the streets and parks, although that's certainly worthwhile in itself. I so admire this independent spirit of getting out and doing something. Instead of soap operas and sedentary retirements, they're out rain or shine, biking and walking and laughing. I love seeing them outside, getting exercise and having fun together.

ONE OF THE LAST STOPS on my route is a city park building that houses programs and classes for neighborhood residents. There's a lot more joking around than actual bending or stretching in the weekly stretching and yoga class for seniors, but at least they're out there. Then they all pile into vehicles, drive one block to the corner bakery, and hang out eating pastries and drinking coffee.

One day when I entered the park building, music of the Big Band era reverberated around the lobby. At first I thought it might be a dance class in the auditorium, but closer listening revealed several notes landing flat or tailing off sharp. I suspected it wasn't a recording. One thing for sure, it was lively and loud!

I don't know the names of those old swing tunes, but they immediately put me in mind of the 1930s or World War II. Les Brown and Glenn Miller.

After delivering the mail to the front desk, I asked where the music was coming from. A young man looked up from his computer terminal and nodded toward the hallway. "There's a bunch of old guys down there practicing."

"Think they'd mind if I looked in on them?"

He laughed. "They probably won't even know you're there."

The sound grew louder and the amateur quality became more apparent as I got closer. A clarinet continually squealed off at the end of phrases. A window in the door allowed a view of several rows of chairs lined up in arcs facing an elderly bandleader. All the band members were men, and a few women, probably wives, stood off to one side.

The audience of women was watching with toe-tapping enthusiasm. It was easy to envision them listening to this same music fifty years ago. Their wavy ringlets had all turned gray, and flashy high heels had been replaced by sensible, wide-soled support shoes, but they still had energy and fun on their faces. They reminded me of a group of teenage girls from my generation hanging around listening to a garage band playing rock and roll.

A quick twist of the doorknob and I ducked inside. The young man at the front desk had been right; nobody seemed to notice my entrance. A double bass threatened to fall over and squash the slender little man plucking away on it. He wore his white hair slicked straight back, and his whole body rocked with the rhythms he produced as his left hand rappelled up and down the neck of the huge instrument.

Two violins, a cello, and several reeds took up the front row; I thought I spotted the squealing clarinet. But brass—trombones, trumpets, and a tuba—constituted the majority of the band, lining the back rows.

The overall effect was a haphazard unison. The bandleader wore a sport coat with trousers that stopped about three inches too short. His gestures were emphatic, the baton and his arms swinging far and wide, but try as he might he could not slow down the momentum of this group of musicians. The song ripped ahead with an energy all its own. Legs bounced out the beat as bodies rocked to the rhythm. A bow tie here, a "proud grandpa" T-shirt there. A dapper, pencil-line thin mustache, and shorts with knee-high socks.

From a technical standpoint, the music really wasn't very good. But it had an undeniable passion. These were the guys that, as young men, had marched off to confront fascism and the Rising Sun. They had charged ahead with an irrepressible fervor. Later, they had built families and industries, and now, in their golden years, they continued to exhibit their independence and a zest for life through their music.

I couldn't stop my foot from tapping any more than I could keep the smile off my face. The whole building struggled to contain the strength and independent spirit of this music. The conductor desperately tried to keep up with his band, the clarinet continued to squeal, toes kept tapping randomly, and the grin on my face grew larger as the music swept me away.

When three trombone players in the middle row suddenly stood up to lead the way through a solo passage, I laughed in delight. It was not a crisp, unified movement for this group. Because of physical infirmities they sort of staggered to their feet. Even the conductor looked startled to see them rising. But I knew the classy image they were going for, and when they once again were seated the women and I spontaneously began clapping.

As far as I know they don't make any public appearances, but once a month when I hear that catchy swing music cascading down the hallway, I pause for a moment to listen and soak up some of their energy.

=✉=

MY INTERACTIONS WITH elderly patrons on my route are many and varied. Sometimes senior citizens who host block parties for National Night Out get a kick out of having the mailman in attendance. On the other hand, I've paid my respects at several

memorial services. Occasionally, I get a chance to help an
elderly patron by mailing letters or buying postage. I push cars
out of snowdrifts a couple of times each winter, and I've even
hauled in a bag or two of groceries. For my part, it's comforting
to know that if I slip on a patch of ice and get hurt, or get sick
and can't go on, there are literally hundreds of people nearby
who are willing to help me.

Like the time I locked myself out of the jeep. The door isn't
supposed to lock without a key, but the mechanism on this
particular vehicle had rattled itself loose. As if in a nightmare, I
watched in slow motion as the little metal knob dropped when
I slid the door shut. The keys still hung from the dashboard
ignition where I had left them. Fortunately, I knew everyone
on the block, so I knocked on the door of the nearest retired
couple, knowing they would be home.

All I wanted was to use their telephone to call my supervisor.
I told them that there were extra sets of keys at the post office,
but the old gentleman of the house would hear nothing of that.
He insisted on helping me. The coat hanger he brought out
was useless. We bent it into all sorts of configurations, but vir-
tually everything on those old jeeps, other than the windows,
is made of metal, so there was nowhere for the coat hanger to
penetrate. But we tried both doors anyhow, and the rear door,
too, and while we worked more neighbors joined us.

I explained to them how sloppy the locking mechanisms are
on the jeeps. In some cases, one key will open several vehicles.
One by one, then, we tried all of our own keys, laughing and
joking our way around the jeep. As we did so, the little group

continued to grow. Someone produced a tiny screwdriver, inserted it into the keyhole, and managed to move the lock, but not quite enough to open it. Of course, after that, everyone had to try his hand with the screwdriver.

Finally, good old common sense and ingenuity shuffled up. "I believe I have just the item to open that lock," the oldest resident on the block proclaimed. His gnarled, arthritic hands rested on the doorframe as he studied my dilemma. We all went silent and looked at the diminutive speaker. He winked at me. "I'll be right back."

Watching him amble down the sidewalk, I worried about all the time I had lost. He lived halfway down the block. The remaining old-timers stood along the curb chatting. It appeared that I was back in that slow-motion nightmare again, and there wasn't much I could do about the situation but let it play itself out.

When the man finally returned, he walked doubled over under the weight of the tool he carried. It turned out to be the largest magnet I had ever seen. It must have weighed seven or eight pounds. "Got it down at the foundry where I used to work," he explained, struggling to hoist it up to the door. For a moment I worried he might drop it. I could imagine explaining to my boss how a gigantic magnet happened to smash through my window.

It kept sticking to the metal door, but with a couple of us lifting, we managed to slide it up the outside of the window. As if by magic, and to a chorus of cheers, the magnet disengaged the small metal latch right through the glass of the window.

When I finally drove away, the guys were still hanging out at the curb, reminiscing about lifetimes of experiences. While I'm sure that the story of using a magnet to get into the mailman's jeep would rate low on their all-time list of creative problem solving, it sure had impressed me.

≡✉≡

OF COURSE, I'VE ALSO encountered seniors who are not so impressive, who show the darker aspects of the life-long racism they have held. A few years ago a severe storm on the Fourth of July blew down tens of thousands of acres of forest in the Boundary Waters Canoe Area Wilderness in northern Minnesota. My wife and I own a cabin nearby, and several patrons asked about damage to our property. Other than half a dozen trees knocked down, we weathered the storm just fine. After the blow-down, the big concern has been the dead trees drying into fuel for a potentially massive forest fire. An older man on my route offered a solution.

"I tell you what they ought to do," Stan commented one morning as we stood on his front stoop.

"What's that?" I asked.

He leaned in confidentially, and said, "They should send a bunch of them Jews up there. They'd figure out a way to make lumber out of all those trees, and probably make a bunch of money off it, too." He stepped back and cackled at what he considered a clever wisecrack.

Swallowing my anger, and with all the nonchalance I could muster, I replied, "Gee, Stan, I'll have to tell my wife about that. She's Jewish, too, you know, so maybe she could get in on some of that action."

Stan's eyes went big and round as he stammered, "Well, you know what I mean."

"Sure, Stan, I know just what you mean. Here's your mail."

I walked off, leaving him to think about it. After that, even though I still talk to him nearly every day, that particular subject has never come up again.

≡✉≡

WHEN I RETURNED FROM a vacation a few years ago, I had more trouble with an elderly patron. He had greeted the African-American letter carrier substituting on my route with racial slurs and told him to stay out of his yard.

I was furious. When I arrived at the man's house I rang the bell and banged on the front door. I had a pretty good hunch he was home, but he refused to come to the door. Unable to vent my anger, I bundled up his mail and took it with me. Day after day for a week I rang the doorbell, then brought his mail back and tossed it in a tub on the floor. There really wasn't any precedent for my behavior. Perhaps I would be in trouble for holding back this fellow's mail, but it seemed as though the lines had been drawn, and until he came forward to answer for his actions, I refused to deliver his mail.

The job of a substitute letter carrier is tough enough without the added burden of dealing with a ranting racist. All letter carriers start out as substitutes. I did it for two and a half years before getting a regular assignment. Every day you're

on a different route, walking through unfamiliar neighborhoods, looking for hidden mailboxes and lurking dogs. Subs
work long days, often doing a whole route and then carrying
overtime mail off a second route. I worked six days a week, at
least ten hours a day, for months at a time. It's a test of endur-
ance. Because of this shared experience, senior carriers look
out for the welfare of substitutes. Whether it's a simple word of
encouragement, advice on dressing for the weather, or a secret
shortcut on a particular route, we try to offer support. In this
case, I intended to back up the substitute by confronting an
incorrigible patron.

Finally, one morning at least a week after my return, a front
window clerk came to get me as I cased mail. She told me a
customer wanted to know why he wasn't getting any deliveries. Maybe the fellow thought I would go easier on him if there
were others around, but it didn't work out that way.

"Where's my mail?" he demanded as I approached the
counter.

"I thought you told the mail carrier to stay out of your yard."

"So? What's that got to do with you?"

"Didn't you tell him not to set foot in your yard again?"
I was really mad now; his sarcasm had pushed all my buttons.
I wanted him to acknowledge out loud, in front of a lobby full
of customers, the real reason why he wasn't getting any mail.

He was so upset he could barely speak. Louder now, and
spluttering belligerently, he demanded, "Where's my mail?"

"You threatened a letter carrier, a friend of mine."

"I didn't threaten anyone. Give me my mail!"

"You said, 'Stay out of my yard, or else.' That sure sounds like a threat to me."

His face was glowing with anger. "Just give me my mail!"

"Why should I? You didn't want it when the sub tried delivering it."

A pause, and then, "I don't want his kind in my yard!"

There. He'd said it, and now an uncomfortable silence fell over the lobby. Customers standing in line looked shocked. The window clerks stood back, warily watching us. Leaning in closer, I lowered my voice. "On his easiest day, that black man works harder than you ever dreamed of working. If you ever threaten him again, I'll have delivery to your house permanently suspended. You'll need to get a post office box if you want any mail." I didn't know if I could actually do that, but he didn't know that, and if he continued running his mouth, I sure would try.

As I turned to go back to work, I told the window clerk where to find the tub of curtailed mail. Several letter carriers had gathered behind me in support, nodding their approval. The substitute carrier was standing there too, looking a little self-conscious. I slapped him on the back as I passed, and that broke the tension. Smiles broke out, the line of customers began to move again, and we all got back to work.

Delivering mail to that man was uncomfortable for a while. I didn't see him for a long time, but finally, as he mowed the lawn in his backyard one afternoon, he waved at me and I nodded. Given a choice, I wouldn't have had it end that way, but I suppose it'll just have to be good enough.

A Snapshot in Time

Taking my break one afternoon in a park near my route, I watched three boys swoop into the parking lot on their bicycles. Shirttails fluttering, they darted across each other's paths, laughing, arms thrown out recklessly. Down the length of the parking lot they flew like a small flock of birds, too much in the moment to notice me.

At the far end they banked into wide turns before racing back. A firm grip and a mighty jerk on the handlebars created the most airtime from two speed bumps. Exhilaration pushed them ever faster and higher. On this, the first day after the last day of the school year, three months of summer vacation must have felt like an eternity of freedom.

From the open door of my postal jeep I watched them careen across the parking lot yet again. At the far end, one of the boys dismounted and grabbed an old board from beside a mound of sand the street department had dumped after the spring street sweeping. He leaned the board against the curb to create a ramp leading out of the parking lot. No sooner was it in place than one of his comrades zoomed in at full speed, launched himself off the ramp, and hurtled himself high up on the pile of sand. They took turns to see who could soar the farthest. It was a fast-paced circus act in which none of the horseplay is scripted, and all the stunts are impromptu.

One of the boys dropped his bike at the side of the sand pile and scampered over to the corner of the parking lot where the park department had placed an outdoor toilet. Instead of going inside, however, he knelt down to reach underneath the enclosed unit. In the meantime, the other two boys left their bikes and took seats against the mound of sand. Jostling and elbowing each other, they squirmed impatiently, flinging handfuls of sand, until their friend returned. He had extracted a magazine from its hiding place under the toilet, and now he took a seat between his two companions.

My postal jeep was the only vehicle in the parking lot. Positioned directly in front of where the boys sat, with my door wide open, I was totally exposed to their view. Even so, I was sure they hadn't noticed me. I felt a little self-conscious at the thought that I might be spying on them, but at the same time I didn't dare move for fear of disturbing their pre-adolescent escapades. So, in the end, I simply watched as they became quietly engrossed in turning the pages of the magazine.

For a few minutes the park became utterly still. It was like plunging into a vacuum. But it wasn't long before I heard a snicker, then a snort. Soon a grimy finger pointed at a picture and all three boys burst out laughing.

Within moments the magazine was safely stashed back

under the toilet. Once again the boys mounted their bikes. The few quiet moments were quickly forgotten as they charged across the parking lot with renewed energy and shouts of delight. They flew past me and continued out of the parking lot, skittering away like leaves blown by the wind.

The Power of the Uniform

Wearing the same outfit to work every day sure makes it easier to get dressed so early in the morning. Even though all letter carriers wear the same uniforms, making us easy to identify on the street, there are subtle differences. For instance, my feet seldom get cold, so all winter I get by with simple rubber galoshes against the snow, while many carriers plod around in heavy felt-lined boots. Because we handle thin pieces of paper all day, mittens are too clumsy, but you'll find about as many styles of gloves in use as there are carriers. I have a partially amputated finger on my left hand that is impossible to keep warm. To get me through the winter, my ingenious wife slit open the seam between two fingers on my glove, sewed them together, and now my short finger rides along in warmth beside my index finger.

Some letter carriers get by with baseball caps all winter, while others use the USPS-issued fake-fur hats with the warm earflaps. We have competitions each spring to see who will be the first to wear shorts out on the route. But all these minor differences aside, the blue letter-carrier uniforms are easily recognized moving through the neighborhood.

≡✉≡

ONE AFTERNOON, A DAY-CARE teacher ran outside, stopped me on the sidewalk, and invited me in to greet her preschool class. Feeling a bit like I had suddenly walked into Mr. Rogers' neighborhood, I entered to find seven or eight children sitting in a circle on the floor. They had made a post office out of a discarded appliance crate. A slot was cut in one wall to accept letters, and a small American flag topped the roof.

After I showed them my uniform, and the key chain with the strange shaped key for opening collection boxes, one student was selected to show me the old leather purse they used as a mail satchel. The long strap hung low off the little girl's shoulder as she demonstrated how she delivered hand-made letters to the other children. Brightly colored, hand-drawn stamps adorned the envelopes, and it was apparent that a lot of work had gone into the writing of numbers and letters.

"I see you're learning your numbers and spelling," I said to the class.

Before I could continue, the little girl with the leather purse piped up, "P is for Penelope!"

Her sudden outburst surprised me, and I smiled down at her. "That's a beautiful name," I said.

She wrapped an arm around my leg and asked, "Mr. Mailman, do you deliver to my house?"

Her perky voice and ringlets transformed Mr. Rogers'

neighborhood into a Shirley Temple movie. She looked up at me with big round eyes, determined that I was her carrier.

"Well, that depends on where you live," I said.

She paused, thinking hard, and said, "I live in Minneapolis."

I couldn't bear to disappoint those adoring eyes, so I said, "In that case, I think I *do* deliver to your house!"

She jumped up and down and clapped her hands. Playing my role to the hilt, I returned after work with some USPS activity books, as well as an extra letter-carrier cap the children could use while delivering their mail. They didn't need the whole uniform. With their imaginations, the old leather purse was as real as my mail satchel. But the cap could still somehow make it all official.

≡✉≡

JUST AS I'M READILY RECOGNIZED in my uniform, I know most of the cars that my patrons drive. I'm constantly hailed on the street with honks and waves. Total strangers spot my uniform and stop me to ask for directions. When Lorraine and her pals return from a garage sale expedition, they often pull over to show off the treasures they've collected.

I enjoy this familiarity; it's a small-town friendliness smack in the middle of the big city. On the other hand, it's interesting to note that when I encounter these same people after hours, without my uniform, they hardly recognize me at all. At the neighborhood coffee shop, or the library, my greetings are often met with blank stares. I even attended a block party one night where everyone in attendance lived on my route. For several minutes I walked around unnoticed before a woman blurted out, "Oh, my God! I know you! You're the mailman, aren't you?"

One time in the grocery store, my wife and I ran into Agnes and her husband Ed, a retired couple I had talked to many times while delivering mail. They ignored my greetings and avoided looking at me. The harder I tried, the more obvious it became that they didn't recognize me. Finally, they hustled their cart down the aisle just to get away. I couldn't let them run off thinking I was some kind of babbling lunatic, so I chased after them, explaining, "I'm your mailman, remember?"

They stopped, took a closer look, and then nearly fell over themselves apologizing. After I introduced them to my wife, we couldn't get away for the longest time. Now I usually don't say anything unless a person recognizes me and says "hello" first. It's just too awkward and difficult.

=✉=

SOME PEOPLE EXPECT MORE out of their letter carrier than the simple delivery of their mail.

"Take this package for me, will you? Here's five bucks for postage. Just leave the change in the mailbox tomorrow."

It should be obvious that letter carriers don't have the time to mail packages for patrons. Besides, we've been warned against handling cash for people out on the street. Most of us will occasionally mail items for elderly shut-ins who have no other option, but that's it.

Another complaint we hear often is, "How come you get

here in the afternoon? I want my mail in the morning."

I try to explain. "The way this route is set up, sir, your delivery is later in the day. There's nothing I can do about it. Not everyone can get their mail at nine in the morning."

"Well, I pay taxes. The way I see it, you guys work for me, and I want an earlier delivery."

Then I have to explain that their taxes have nothing to do with the Postal Service. We're an independent federal agency. The Postal Service is part of the executive branch of the federal government, but the postmaster general hasn't been a member of the presidential cabinet since 1970. Through the sale of postage we raise our own operating funds. However, because of this pseudo-government connection, and our daily service to the American public, letter carriers are often asked to perform above and beyond the line of duty.

One of the toughest demands I ever faced occurred when I came upon the scene of an accident. I had heard the squealing tires. Witnesses shouted for help. Several people dialed 911, and dozens of pedestrians and homeowners gathered around. But as I approached the scene, I was the one ushered to the side of the elderly woman who had been struck by a car. The crowd made room for me to pass through, as if my uniform automatically qualified me to lend assistance. Somehow I became the one to sit in the street with her.

I held her cold hands in mine. She wasn't a resident of my route. I found out later that she lived less than half a mile away. She had been to the bank to buy traveler's checks for a tour to Norway, the first overseas trip of her life. As she walked home, a car had run a red light and hit her in the crosswalk.

Now it was stopped in the middle of the intersection. The driver stalked around it in a fit of anguish. "I killed her!" he wailed, slapping at his head and grabbing his hair. Punching the trunk of the car, he yelled, "I can't believe this! I killed her. I just know it. It's all my fault. I killed her!"

"Will somebody get him out of here?" I called to the crowd. Two men immediately corralled him and led him around to the far side of the car.

"Ambulance is on the way!" someone shouted.

The woman opened her eyes, but they didn't focus on anything. I leaned closer, offering words of comfort. Seconds later, her eyes rolled back, and I thought this was the end.

"Don't go away!" I pleaded. "Stay here. Talk to me."

Time and again we did this. Each time seemed to be the last. I kneaded her cold hands and stroked her bare arms.

"Where's that damn ambulance?" I yelled. By now the crowd was overflowing the intersection. Traffic was blocked off. Where had all these people come from? And why was I the one sitting in the middle of the street?

"Paramedics are sixty seconds away," someone called. Now the siren was audible. "I have a patch-through to the ambulance driver," a man said, stepping up to offer me his cell phone.

For a fleeting moment I wondered how a person should answer a phone with a dispatched ambulance driver on the other end of the line.

"Hello," I said, much louder than necessary, trying to cover my shaky nerves.

"Is the victim conscious?"

"Not really. She's sort of in and out of it."

"Try to keep her awake. Is she bleeding?"

"Not that I can see."

"Okay. We're thirty seconds out. Can you cover her? Keep her warm?"

It was at least eighty-five degrees outside. Sweat trickled off my brow into my eyes, but I assumed that shock was the real worry here. The woman's hands were ice cold. "Anybody got a blanket?" I called to the crowd.

Within seconds we were deluged with blankets, beach towels, and sweaters.

Her eyes opened again as I covered her. A glint of light appeared, and I thought she actually looked at me. "You're going to be okay," I lied. "Help is just seconds away."

Then her eyes rolled back to a ghostly white stare. This time she really seemed gone. Squeezing her hands as hard as I could, I pleaded, "Please, don't go away! Not after all this. Don't you dare die on me!"

A paramedic nudged me out of the way. Her lifeless hands flopped to the street as I let them go. I staggered through the crowd. That final vision haunted me for days.

One morning a few days later I overheard a fellow carrier describing how a car had hit a "dear old patron" on his route. I knew it had to be the same woman. Through him, I learned that she survived, although doctors had to put her in a coma for two weeks to protect her brain. Months later she was home, telling her letter carrier all about her injuries—and her revised tour plans. Within a year, the seventy-year-old woman completed her long-delayed journey to Norway. I've never seen her again, although I probably wouldn't recognize her if I did. That first meeting was enough for me.

=✉=

FOR A WEEK OR SO around Christmas I augment my uniform with a Santa Claus hat and beard. The little kids have a blast with that, and most of their parents enjoy it, too. One year I wore a full Santa outfit on Christmas Eve Day. Fortunately, it was cold enough to warrant the extra layer of clothing.

Santa Claus seems to bring out the child in all of us, and many adults get into the spirit of it, too. They greet me with a "Good morning, Santa!" whether they have children at home or not. The Santa hat and beard brings smiles to their faces and a bit of cheer to the neighborhood. But the little children are the ones who really make it great. They stand at the door, excitement pulsing through them, too shy to actually say anything. It's even better, should I happen to have a package for them.

"Thank you, Santa," they say timidly, eyes full of wonder.

Then I have to tell them, "I'm not really Santa Claus, you know. I'm just his helper. But the next time I see him, I'll tell him what a great kid you are."

The excitement bubbles over then, and words tumble out of even the shyest ones, joyful at meeting Santa's helper. I have to admit, though, it's twice as much fun for me.

=✉=

ONE SUMMER DAY the rumble of an approaching Harley-
Davidson broke through my midday musings as I delivered
mail. A full-dressed police motorcycle was leading a funeral
procession. Warning lights flashed on either side of the wind-
shield, with another one rotating from a post extending off the
rear fender. The uniformed officer raced into the intersection
to secure it for the long line of cars that followed.

Whenever I see motorcycle cops I'm compelled to watch
them pass, perhaps because they seem like a throwback to a less
complicated era in history and law enforcement. Or, more likely,
it's simply because there aren't that many of them around anymore. With flashing lights and deep-throated engines, polished
chrome and glistening paint, starched uniforms, a heavy brass
badge, and law enforcement insignia on the shoulders, you have
the classic picture of police power and prestige.

The motorcycle sped into the intersection, stopping at an
angle to face crossing traffic. A knee-high boot stepped out
to support the bike. Dark aviator-style sunglasses peered out
from beneath a short black visor on the helmet. An Adam's
apple bobbed as a gloved hand rose to halt oncoming traffic.
Only one vehicle approached, driven by a young man I recognized from my route.

Still a teenager, Darryl had been driving for only a couple of
years. He used the old family car to attend a nearby two-year
college. Slouched low in the seat, his head barely rising above
the dashboard, he held the steering wheel in one hand while
heavy bass notes reverberated from his stereo.

I had known Darryl throughout his entire school career.

When he was in high school, his parents and I worried a little about some of his friends. They were a tough bunch, and it seemed for a while as though Darryl might take a wrong turn. But, as his father and I commented in a recent conversation, it appeared the worst was over. Darryl still liked to dress down, and the old family car looked like a junker under his care, but he went to school every day, and his father told me he thought Darryl was showing an interest in a career in business.

I followed the young man's line of sight back to the motorcycle cop, who was preparing to motor off to secure another intersection. Just then, Darryl pulled away from the stop sign. He turned in front of the cop, trying to get ahead of the procession. Why he waited so long, I don't know, but darting out ahead of the motorcycle was a bad idea.

Not seeing him right away, the police officer started off, then dodged toward the curb to avoid sideswiping Darryl's car. The next instant he shot forward, and I've never seen a cop so angry.

"Pull over!" he screamed at the kid. He took but a second to overtake the car. Waving wildly, he motioned to the curb. "Pull that car over. Now!" he bellowed.

Darryl went pale with fear. He sat up straight, both hands on the wheel, and diligently maneuvered to the side. The police officer leaped off the motorcycle to lambaste him at the driver's window.

"Are you crazy? What's wrong with you?" the cop demanded. "Of all the stupid things to do—you could have killed me!"

Showing a little sense at last, Darryl kept his mouth shut.

Furious, the cop reached through the window, grabbed the kid by the shirt, and yanked him up face to face. Even from across the street I could hear every word.

"You stupid fool! I ought to haul your ass in and lock you up!"

The funeral hearse passed them then, effectively interrupting the barrage of insults. Looking around, the officer realized he had to leave. Turning back to the kid, he said, "You wait right here. Understand me? You sit right here until I get back. You move so much as an inch, I'll throw the book at you."

With that, he remounted the motorcycle. Before racing off, he pointed a gloved finger at Darryl, and yelled, "Not one inch!" Then he tore off, whipping up a cloud of sand and pebbles.

From my angle at the corner I watched the young man as the funeral procession passed. He slowly slouched down again, probably out of embarrassment this time. Even after the last car passed he remained sitting there. I considered the situation, and realized he had quite the dilemma on his hands. The whole incident had happened so quickly. I never saw the police officer take note of the license plate, or even the make or model of Darryl's car. There hadn't been time. In all likelihood then, the cop had no way of ever tracking him down.

I also knew that a funeral procession heading this way meant burial at Fort Snelling National Cemetery. That was at least four or five miles away. By the time his escort duties were finished, the police officer could very well have forgotten the whole incident. Maybe his threat had simply been a bluff.

On the other hand . . .

I crossed the street to work my way back down the other side. After all that commotion, complete silence hung over the neighborhood. Even the car's radio was turned off. He never looked at me, didn't seem to even notice me passing. I wondered if he was considering the two horns of his dilemma, or if he was just too scared to move. Either way, when I returned to my jeep at the end of the block, he was still parked there by the side of the road.

A couple of hours later, after finishing my route, I detoured through the intersection on my way back to the post office. Darryl's car was still parked at the curb, the young man sitting in the shade on the lawn nearby. He had made his choice.

I talked to his parents a few days later. His father told me that he had spotted the car on his way home from work. This was late in the afternoon, several hours after the cop had left. Thinking his son had car trouble, he stopped to help. The kid confessed the whole story to him.

"He sat there all afternoon," the father recounted with a grin. "Five hours or more. When I said, 'Let's go home,' he shook his head, and said, 'No way.' I had to call the police to dispatch a squad car. A cop talked to him, gave him a lecture, then sent him home."

"He didn't get a ticket or anything?"

"Nope. But he sure learned a lesson."

Darryl went on to finish school, although the old family car didn't last that long. He's married now and manages a home improvement store in the suburbs. On a day shortly before last Christmas, I encountered Darryl and his wife at his folks' house. An infant lay curled in his arms when they greeted me at the door. Darryl grinned at the sight of my Santa hat and beard.

"I hoped you'd wear it," he said. "I remember as kids we'd always watch for you during Christmas break."

Pulling off a glove, I reached out to tickle the baby's chin. A toothless smile grinned back at me. I guess you just never know the effect a uniform will have on a person.

The American Dream

Several years ago I met Michael, a young man who had pur-
chased a small house on my route. The structure was in dire
need of repairs. He set to work on it, and over time we dis-
cussed his progress with plumbing, electrical, and painting.
He was single and handy, and I enjoyed his perplexity over
curtains and flowerpots while admiring his prowess installing
new doors and windows.

Minneapolis has thousands of wonderful early to mid-
twentieth-century dwellings—solid bungalows and sturdy
wooden frame structures built to withstand the capricious
nature of our northern climate. It's fascinating to watch them
being cared for and restored. This particular post-and-beam
structure, built in 1906, went through a dramatic restoration
after Michael moved in. A contractor was brought in to work
on the major exterior components, while Michael continued
his slow but steady progress with the living spaces.

At the outset, the old house seemed to sag and slouch under
the great weight of its years. That was understandable when I

saw four old roofs torn off, as well as three layers of siding. At least one of the layers of siding contained high levels of asbestos, and the contractor showed me the heavy black plastic liner in the dumpster used to contain the carcinogenic fibers.

"Every night we close that bag off to seal in the asbestos," he said, pointing at the dumpster. "I'll be glad when we can finally get it out of here."

"Me, too," I thought.

Within a few short weeks a new roof was installed, as well as lightweight vinyl siding. The house now seemed to stand taller and straighter with all that weight removed. It looked lighter and healthier, like a person getting back into shape by dieting and working out.

As repairs progressed, Michael told me how dissatisfied he had become with his job. He was employed as a diesel mechanic in a local shop, and his boss called him out at all hours of the night to make emergency repairs on trucks passing through the metro area. "I know how much they're billing for my work," he complained to me one time. "But I still get the same old hourly wage."

Knowing how hard he worked, I suggested, "Why don't you start your own business?"

He snorted. "Yeah, right. Do you know how expensive all that equipment is? They have me over a barrel. I could never afford to go it alone."

But I knew he was thinking about it, and probably had been since long before I mentioned it, because one day he just up and quit his job. He posted his name and phone number at all the truck stops and wayside rest areas within range. At home and in his pickup truck, he installed CB radios to take calls at all hours of the day.

He started small, working out of his truck. The next year he added a big trailer for hauling more tools, parts, and tires. Salvaged truck parts began appearing on his porch. Most of these he was able to recondition and use in repairs. Business kept building.

One morning he came home as I was delivering his mail. His coveralls were filthy, covered with grease and torn at the knees. He looked exhausted, but when I greeted him a broad smile blossomed across his face.

"Been out all night," he said.

"Are you sorry you took the plunge?"

"No way. These over-the-roaders will pay anything to keep their rigs running. They're all on tight schedules, and when they need help, they usually need it right now."

He laughed while inspecting his blackened hands. "If I can scrub some of this grunge off, I hope to do some paperwork, then maybe get a nap."

One day I noticed a school bus parked in front of his house. Perched on a ladder, Michael operated a power grinder, sanding off the orange paint. "You work on school buses, too?" I asked.

"Nope. This baby is mine." Climbing down from the ladder, he added, "Come look in the back door."

The rear bumper had been extended, and onto it had been bolted a huge steel vise. When he opened the back door, I saw that all the passenger seats had been removed.

"This is my new shop on wheels. I can haul all my tools and plenty of spare parts. I'm converting some of the wiring to run power tools. What do you think of it?"

"Amazing," was all I could say.

The handfuls of mail he received every day told me that checks were coming in from trucking companies all over the country. He always left his outgoing mail for me to take: hand-addressed envelopes to firms far and wide. Business was steady and continuing to grow.

After a while, a wife was added to the picture, and more recently a son. I always smile to see the old bus bumping through the neighborhood. One thing that hasn't changed, however, is the dirty coveralls.

"I buy them at the second-hand store," he explained one time. "They're impossible to clean, so I wear them until they're shot, then I throw them away. They only cost a couple of bucks, so it's cheaper than trying to clean them."

His wife does the books now, so he's getting more sleep. She even learned CB lingo to take calls. A large addition has been added to the back of the house, and a two-and-a-half stall garage has replaced the old dilapidated one-car structure. His little enterprise is a great success story.

Late on a cold winter night I stopped at a neighborhood convenience store to gas up before going home. Inside the store, I was surprised when a transient warming himself at the coffee machine turned out to be my friend the mechanic.

"Got another call?" I asked.

"Yeah. I've been running all day." From his grime-darkened

face flashed the smooth white grin. "It never fails. On the coldest nights the calls back up." He toasted me with a twenty-four-ounce cup of coffee. "This should get me through."

"Maybe you need to hire an apprentice, or take on a partner," I said.

"Been thinking about that," he said, heading toward the cashier.

He wore black coveralls, which hid most of the dirt, but I could see how they bagged out at the knees. One of the back pockets was torn and hung down his leg like a piece of shedding skin. I thought they must be nearing retirement to the trashcan. A wool stocking cap stretched down low over his forehead, and fingerless gloves revealed his grimy fingernails and hands. The leather on his steel-toed boots was worn off in front, exposing the steel plates underneath.

He shuffled up to the cashier, placed the coffee on the counter, and began digging inside the coveralls for his wallet. The woman looked him up and down, then glanced outside at the icy crystals blowing past the window. Her expression softened when she again looked at my friend, and she reached out to pat his hand gently. "It's okay," she said softly. "You don't have to pay."

Not Quite Lost and Found

One warm summer day, a large, unfamiliar dog suddenly appeared at my side. I was startled, but he didn't act aggressive or nervous. He simply walked up at an angle from the street and fell into stride beside me. He wore a collar and tags, but I had two fists full of mail, so I continued on my way, intending to look at his ID when my hands were free.

When I stopped to put mail in a slot, he paused and waited beside me. If I took more than a few seconds, he quietly sat down and surveyed the neighborhood around us. He seemed to pay no particular attention to anything, either by sniffing or "marking." He was simply out for a walk, and apparently he had decided to share it with me for a while.

In a way it was flattering, the way he waited for me. With the neighborhood under his constant surveillance, I had my own canine bodyguard. He stood tall and slender, with the gray and white markings of a husky. There was an athletic elegance in his movement, a confidence in his light-footed stride, leaving no doubt that he was quite capable of taking care of himself.

With my hands finally free, I sat on the front steps of a corner house and whistled him closer. He came to me without a moment's hesitation. His tags told me that his name was Wolf, and he lived four or five blocks off my route.

Over the years I've brought many dogs home. Most of them lived on my route and knew me, so they were willing to jump into my jeep for a ride home. One black lab could open the gate to his yard if it wasn't secured with a pin through the latch. When I brought him home, he sat high atop the trays of mail, holding his thick Labrador bulk as steady as possible to avoid falling from his perch. He seemed to study our route, his big black head swiveling to inspect every object we passed. I imagined him thinking, "Well, duh! So *this* is where I turned wrong and got lost!"

I sat on the front steps of the house petting Wolf. With his quiet disposition I got the distinct impression that he wasn't lost at all. He knew exactly where his house was, and he was visiting with me of his own volition. I had to decide if I should try to get him in my jeep for a ride home. The Postal Service wasn't paying me to rescue lost dogs, especially if it required leaving my route to do so.

On the other hand, the neighborhood wouldn't tolerate a dog running loose for too long. Animal Control would be notified, and I didn't want Wolf to have to endure that humiliation.

Just then the front door behind me opened and the lady of the house emerged. "I see you have some company today," she said.

I laughed. Jingling the dog tags, I said, "His name is Wolf. I

guess he decided to join me for a walk. I'm trying to decide if I
dare drive him home."

"Where does he live?"

I had talked to Jeanie many times, so I knew she had lost
her own dog about a year earlier to old age and cancer. She
was a kind person, with an abiding love of animals. An adult
daughter had just moved back in with her.

"He lives just a few blocks away," I said. "Maybe half a mile
at the most."

Wolf suddenly stood up and climbed the steps. He gently
nuzzled Jeanie, rubbing against her legs like a cat. She
scratched his ears while looking at his tag. "There's a phone
number here. If you want, I'll call the owners to come over and
get him. He can wait inside with me."

Thanking her for her generosity, I got up to leave. She
opened the door, and Wolf sauntered in like he owned the
place. I walked away knowing that he would be safe and pro-
vided for.

The next day, Jeanie met me at the door. "They sent a
couple of their kids over to get him," she informed me. "Did
you know there are five children in that household? I guess
they leave the gate open all the time, especially when they're
playing outside in the summer."

She glanced up the block before returning her attention to
me. "I tell you what, though. That Wolf is the nicest dog. Made
no fuss at all while he was here." She lowered her voice, adding,
"I think he kind of liked the peace and quiet after those ram-
bunctious children." I left her standing on the stoop. There had

been a hint of sadness in her voice, which I chalked up to the memory of her old dog.

A few days after my unscheduled meeting with Wolf, I encountered another surprise. At Jeanie's house, sitting in the sunshine on the front steps, was the big gray and white husky. He bowed his head to me, and gave one friendly wag of his tail. I sat down next to him and patted his head.

"What are you doing here?" I asked. He seemed very content, like he enjoyed the sun on his face and the warmth reflecting off the concrete steps. I reached behind me and rapped on the door.

Now it was my turn to say, "Looks like you've got company, Jeanie." A wonderful smile spread across her face when she saw Wolf. His tail wagged several times at the sight of her.

Ultimately, Wolf moved in full time. His family decided it was easier to visit him at Jeanie's rather than drag him home every couple of days. So, in the end, while I guess it wouldn't be accurate to say that Wolf had ever been truly lost, it certainly could be said that someone had found him.

≡✉≡

GUS WAS AN OLD schnauzer mixed-breed who belonged to Karl, a retired letter carrier who lived on my route. Karl had been retired for more years than I had worked for the post office. Every now and then he came outside to discuss the latest changes in the job. One day while Karl and I stood at his door talking, Gus shot outside and hurled himself down the steps. He tore a direct line across the front yard into the street. I looked up at Karl, thinking maybe he should call out to him, but he just stood there, calmly watching his dog beat a straight-line path away from us. With no fences to impede his progress, Gus ran full speed through yards and alleys, never breaking course or his short-legged stride, until he was finally lost from sight.

"Geez, Karl, I'm really sorry," I said, still stunned by the emphatic way in which Gus had made his escape.

"Well, don't worry about it," Karl replied, resignation lending a sigh to his voice. "He runs away whenever he can. He'll go all the way to the freeway where that tall fence stops him. Then he'll run back and forth looking for a way through. He'll tire out soon enough. I'll just drive over there in a few minutes and pick him up."

I tried to make light of it. "At least he's getting some exercise."

Karl smiled. "You know, that dog hates me. He belonged to my wife, and I promised I'd take care of him after she was gone. But he acts like he's in a prisoner of war camp. Maybe he blames me for her death, I don't know. He used to sit in my wife's lap when we watched TV, but now he lies in the corner watching me, like he's plotting his next opportunity to escape."

It was like Steve McQueen in *The Great Escape*, riding his motorcycle along the barbwire fence looking for an escape route from the Nazi prison camp. And in the same way that Steve McQueen was always captured and returned to prison, Gus was always picked up at the freeway fence and brought home.

=✉=

Two SMALL, WHITE, poodle-looking dogs came yapping along the sidewalk like a miniature wolf pack on a hot scent. One stopped to sniff while the other one shot out ahead, then they traded places, attacking and investigating every little object in their path.

I was surprised when they eagerly jumped into my jeep without any coaxing. They wore collars and tags, but because of their energetic and skittish antics, I wanted to have them safely corralled before trying to learn where they lived. Fortunately, their address was only three or four houses off my route.

By the time I pulled up in front of their house, both dogs were sitting in my lap. I guess they were accustomed to riding in vehicles. When I looked at their house, sure enough, I spotted the side gate standing ajar. Then it took some tricky maneuvers to extricate myself from the jeep without letting the dogs out to run away again.

I don't know what I was expecting when I rang the doorbell, but I got a real shock when the owner filled up the doorway. He was enormous, with a belly hanging out over the elastic waistband of his sweat pants. A dingy grayish-white T-shirt couldn't quite hold him all in.

The thought of this huge man living with the two little high-strung poodles suddenly struck me as comical. To avoid laughing, I turned to point at the jeep and asked, "Are those your dogs?"

They were standing on my seat looking out the window at us, happily yapping and bouncing.

"Why, those little devils," the man said, coming through the door.

For a moment, then, I had a real bad feeling. He glanced at the open gate as his long strides propelled him swiftly toward the jeep. I had to jog to stay ahead of him. Would he hurt the dogs for trying to run away?

I slid the door open with the thought that if they took off again, I would let them go. Before I could react, however, the two little balls of fur catapulted from the seat into the man's outstretched arms. They licked his wide chin as he snuggled his face into their fur. "You little rascals," he bellowed. "What am I going to do with you? Don't you know you could've gotten hurt? Or stolen?"

He turned on his heel and carried them up to the house, mumbling bits of baby talk and ignoring me. But that was okay. The dogs were safely home again, my fears were unwarranted, and I could go on with my day.

=✉=

SATURDAY MORNINGS CAN be pretty quiet in a residential neighborhood. With no businesses nearby attracting traffic, without the roar of school buses on the weekend, and with parents and their children sleeping in, I often spend the first hour or so on my route walking through a virtual ghost town. Shades are pulled, and newspapers still lie at the front door steps. It's a good time for me to inspect unique varieties of shrubs and perennials or discover new ideas for decks and gardens. I pass peacefully across the deserted lawns, lost in my own thoughts and daydreams.

A few years ago I was startled out of one of these Saturday

morning reveries by the sudden appearance of a young woman at her front door. Still in her robe, she clutched an oversized mug of coffee in both hands. I had talked to her and her husband many times, and we had become good friends. Finding them up and about on a Saturday morning was a rarity.

"You wouldn't believe what happened to us last night," she said as she stepped outside to talk. Her conversational voice is always loud and demonstrative.

Bloodshot eyes peered at me from under her dyed black hair, which was in dire need of a brush. I smiled and said, "Well, it looks to me like you had a good time."

"Oh, it started out just fine," she replied with a grin. "Dinner and a few drinks. Heard a great new band down on the West Bank. We got home about midnight." She paused and frowned. "Then, after we went to bed, someone stole our car. Can you believe it?"

I knew her car, a ten-year-old dented rust bucket, and the only thing hard to believe was that anyone would even consider stealing it. But I kept a straight face. "You're kidding! Where was it parked?"

"Right out front here. I did the driving last night, and you know I hate parking in the garage."

The truth of the matter was they never parked in the garage. It was so full of car parts and old furniture that there was no way anyone could have parked a car in there.

"Did you call the police?"

"Yeah. They've already been here and gone. They said they'd probably find it, but no guarantees about what kind of condition it would be in."

"Well, I'm really sorry," I said. "It's just so hard to believe someone would steal a car from right in front of your house. And right under that street light."

"The cop told us that with a screwdriver a car thief can break into a car, start it up, and drive off faster than I can using my key."

The whole episode seemed implausible to me. After all, this was a relatively crime-free neighborhood. A person would have to be mighty desperate to steal a beat-up old car like that one. Her husband joined us, and as they told me about the band they had seen the night before, my gaze wandered past them over a hill down on the next block. I could just make out the roofline of a car. It caught my eye because it seemed to be parked at an odd angle to the curb.

"Hold on a second," I said, stepping up between them on the top step to get a better view down the street. The color was right, and it appeared to be a full-size sedan like theirs. I descended the steps and began walking toward the lip of the hill and the car beyond. "That sure looks like your car down there," I called over my shoulder to them.

It was. Wearing their pajamas and bathrobes, they followed me down the street. We found the gearshift in *neutral* instead of *park*. After rolling across the intersection and downhill for half a block, the car had jumped the curb and come to rest against a boulevard tree. The impact had been slight, the damage minor, especially in light of the normal decrepit appearance of the car.

We sure had fun teasing her about it, though, and even the cops had a good laugh when they returned to close the case.

=✉=

I FOUND ANOTHER ITEM one day that wasn't exactly lost, either, but had far more serious potential consequences. I had returned to my jeep after delivering a block of mail and found an extremely upset little boy. Next to him was the smallest two-wheeled bicycle I had ever seen. The training wheels looked like they belonged on a toy truck. As I drew near, his sobbing howls escalated in volume and intensity. He was anxiously watching me, and I sensed that his performance was intended to attract and hold my attention. Strapped over his shoulder was a school backpack. Tears streamed down his chubby black cheeks as he clung with both hands to the bicycle.

"Hello, young man," I said, walking past him to the back of my jeep. A fresh round of wailing erupted. I took off my satchel and stuffed it inside. Turning to face him, I squatted down to be closer to his size, but kept my distance. I had never seen this child before. I wanted to help him, but I needed to avoid any sort of action that could somehow be misconstrued as improper. While I'm walking my route, there are eyes everywhere. Even when I haven't seen or talked to anyone for a couple of hours, people make note of my passing. The last thing I wanted was for someone down the block, glancing out their window, to misread my intentions or motives. But the poor kid was crying his eyes out. He wasn't faking this fear, and right now all I wanted to do was wrap him up in a bear hug and reassure him that everything would be okay.

"What's your name, little buddy?" I asked, forcing cheerfulness. Many people are more open and trusting around someone in a uniform, but this little fellow was just too upset for that. After pausing briefly to catch his breath, he began howling again, although not nearly as loud as before. His big brown eyes never left me.

I told him my name. "I'm the mailman around here. I sure would like to help you if you'd let me."

Deep sobs interspersed with hiccups.

"Do you live around here?"

Finally, a timid nod. His face was drenched with tears and snot. I opened the door again and was startled by the immediate resumption of ear-splitting wails. I grabbed a tissue and quickly shut the door. Taking a few steps toward him, I dropped to one knee and held the tissue out to him. "Here you go, pal. Use this to wipe off your face." I should have known there was no way he would let go of the bike. His bicycle and backpack were the only familiar items remaining to him, and he clung to them for dear life. But I had no intention of getting any closer to wipe his face off. It turned out to be sort of a standoff, with the white tissue suspended between us. I finally gave up.

We were at the far back edge of my route. I knew everybody for several blocks in front of us, so I assumed he lived in the other direction. I pointed over his shoulder. "Do you live over that way?"

It took a moment for him to nod. Then he tried to speak. "Mom," hiccup, hiccup. "My mom," hiccup. Deep, shuddering gasps.

"Your mother. Is she home?"

His head wagged sideways, then he blurted, "I don't know where she is!"

"Can you show me where you live?"

He nodded before reciting his address. It came out with a deliberate enunciation, like a student giving an answer on an oral exam. His house was just a few blocks away, but he had crossed at least one busy street to get here.

It seemed my options were few, especially since I was afraid he'd start crying again if I even looked away from him. I did not dare load him and his bike into the jeep. Besides, I didn't think he would trust me that far. Where were all the nosy neighbors now, and why didn't someone step outside to see what all the commotion was about?

"I'm five years old."

The soft voice caught me by surprise. What was this, a glimmer of rationality? The tear-stained face looked up at me with trust and hope. His fingers nervously kneaded the grips on the handlebars.

"Five years old?" I echoed. "My goodness, are you in school?" He nodded.

"What school do you go to?"

"Morris Park."

That was good to know, because it was nearby, and if his mother didn't show up maybe they could help me. I was still considering options when he said, "My name is Jermaine."

Again I was surprised by his candid offer of information. But then it occurred to me that a five year old has a very limited repertoire of solid facts. This kid was all alone and couldn't find his mother, but he was giving me everything he knew in an effort to do the right thing.

"My mom's name is Danielle."

That one nearly melted my heart.

"Okay, Jermaine. That's great. You're five years old and you go to Morris Park School. Your mom's name is Danielle. You even know your address. You must be the smartest kid in your class."

He started to smile, but got serious again real quick. "I'm only in kindergarten."

"Kindergarten?" I exclaimed. "That's my favorite!"

Now I got the smile.

"So, this is what we're going to do, Jermaine. I want you to listen real good, because we have to have a plan, right?"

A nod.

"Good. Now, I want you to ride your bicycle, and I'm going to drive my jeep." A shadow of fear crossed his face, so I quickly added, "But we won't split up, okay? I'll just drive along beside you." I had no idea how I would pull that off, but I couldn't let this kid start crying again.

I pointed down the street in the direction we would be going. "You stop at each corner and wait for me, Jermaine. I don't want you crossing any streets unless I'm right next to you, okay?"

His foot was already on the pedal when he nodded at me.

We started off slowly. The tiny wheels of the bike prevented him from going very fast, but he pedaled for all he was worth. When we got to a busier street, I had to speed up a bit because of traffic. Locating him in the side view mirror took a moment, but when I found him, I immediately veered back to the curb. He stood in the middle of the sidewalk straddling his bicycle. I threw open my door to hear him screaming, "Don't leave me! Don't leave me!"

"I won't leave you, Jermaine. I'm right here."

Fighting through the tears he got back on his bike. After that, I turned on my hazard lights and idled along the curb to stay next to him. Jermaine kept a constant watch on me. I realized that to a casual observer this might look improper, that perhaps the mailman was up to no good, but people could think whatever they wanted. Jermaine had been through enough already, and I wasn't going to abandon him.

Once we got moving again it took only a few minutes to reach his house. We pulled up in front of a modest dwelling with the telltale signs of a resident child: a deflated basketball in the yard and action figure stickers in the window. Jermaine watched as I climbed the steps to ring the doorbell.

Getting no response at the door, I asked him, "Do you have any friends in the neighborhood?"

He shook his head.

"How about neighbors? Do you know any of your neighbors?"

Negative. "My mom might."

Coming down the steps I decided to check the backyard. "Wait here, Jermaine. I'm going to try the back door. I'll be right back, okay?"

With no luck in the backyard, either, I had to decide which neighbor's house to approach. That's the other thing about a letter carrier's uniform; complete strangers will open their doors to talk to you, and the time had come to enlist some help so I could get back to work.

But now there was a taxi parked behind my jeep, its back door hanging open. Jermaine was in the arms of the woman I knew must be named Danielle. Both were in tears, even though Jermaine was bawling his mother out for leaving him all alone. He was really mad, and I couldn't blame him.

On my way to the jeep, I told her how proud she should be of her son. "He's a smart kid," I told her, bringing on a fresh round of tears. "He figured out what he needed to do to take care of himself."

She explained that her car had broken down, and she had to get a tow truck and a cab. She had been worried sick about not being home when her son returned from school. For his part, Jermaine wouldn't let go of her and didn't look back at me. Even though he hadn't really been lost, I was glad he'd found me.

I've never spoken to him again. He's much older now, and I see him walking through my route or shooting hoops in the schoolyard with his buddies. He never waves or acknowledges me, but when our eyes meet, I know he remembers.

A Cup of Coffee

Snow had started falling around dinnertime the day before. Big fat flakes, without a wind to disturb the soft edges of accumulation. Coming down in thick swirls, it alighted so gently and swiftly you would swear you could see it pile up. By mid-morning of the next day, eight or ten inches of new snow redefined the landscape. The sun came out, sparkling with an eye-piercing brilliance off the glittering white surface.

Delivering the mail that morning was like walking in loose sand. Icy granules of snow packed down underfoot, then slid out from beneath my boots, making each step a lung-busting challenge. By lunchtime I was exhausted. Breaking new trail is hard work, and I still had four or five hours of walking ahead of me. My pace slowed. Instead of simply struggling and pushing through it, however, I decided to try to admire the beauty of the wintry landscape.

All the classic winter snow scenes appeared: cedar fence rails and posts bearing a delicate mantle of snow; dark green boughs of pine and balsam weighed down under fresh white drifts, occasionally revealing the brilliant red flash of a cardinal. A small charcoal grill, neglected for the winter on a front stoop, became a rocket ship with its cone head capsule of snow. Other items lost their identities altogether, indiscriminate lumps under the thick white blanket.

At one point I spotted a strange imprint in the snow near a row of bushes. A large bird, perhaps a hawk or owl of some sort, had scooped up a morsel of food. Individual feathers from the tips of the raptor's outstretched wings marked the snow. From the impressive length of the wingspan, and the depth of the feathered imprints, I deduced that he must have been struggling as hard as I was in the snow. I could almost feel his exertion as he tried to pull himself back aloft.

The harsh scraping of shovels on concrete broke the snow's hush. Plodding along, I came upon a trio of snow shovelers near the far end of the block. I had never seen the workers before. They must have been hired to shovel, but that seemed odd, because all the usual snow-removal outfits used plows or snowblowers. An enterprising youngster might earn some extra cash shoveling for neighbors, but these three were adults. They wouldn't make much profit clearing snow by hand. Their old pickup truck, a rusty, dented, road-salt-encrusted wreck, was parked near the corner.

Drawing near, I saw there were two men and a woman, all with the long, shiny black hair of Native Americans. One of the men appeared to be too old and overweight for the physical strain. He took short breaks between scoops to catch his breath. The way he leaned forward, using the shovel for support, betrayed his age and discomfort. Even though the temperature was below freezing, none of them wore hats or gloves, and the big man's coat hung open. When he spotted me, I groaned and looked away.

I felt him coming up the sidewalk behind me as I put mail in the slot. When I turned around, he greeted me with a broad grin and a glint of humor in his eyes. "*Aaniin niiji,*" he said. "Hello, my friend."

Heavy swaths of gray hair along his temples and deep wrinkles at the corners of his eyes showed him to be even older than I had imagined. I resigned myself to the inevitable request I had been expecting. He surprised me by asking, "Hey, my friend, do you have an aspirin?"

If he was trying to make a living by shoveling snow, I had no doubt that he was in desperate need of aspirins. I looked at his companions, leaning on their shovels and watching for my response.

His expression was open and sincere. I wished I did have some aspirins to give him. But I had to reply, "Sorry, I don't have any with me."

If anything, the old man's good-natured smile grew even larger. "Well," he said, "it was worth a try." He waved an arm across the neighborhood. "Walking through all this snow, I thought you might have some."

His voice was soft but resonated with a depth of character. With that and his impressive size and bearing, he could have been a leader of men had he so chosen. Perhaps he was.

Showing no inclination to leave, he repositioned his hands

over the top of the shovel handle. His partners resumed working, and I took a moment to look at them. The woman was of an indeterminate middle age, with a tough look about her, as though life hadn't always been kind to her. The other fellow was much younger and looked downright mean. But then, anyone with a tattoo on his face looks intimidating to me. The three of them were just the most improbable looking crew for a job like this.

The old man drew a deep sigh. I thought about offering him a couple dollars to buy some aspirins, but he hadn't actually asked for money, and I didn't want to offend him. I was puzzled, however, as to how they happened to be here shoveling snow. They certainly weren't from around here.

I turned to move on, wishing I had something encouraging to say to complement the old man's friendly smile. The thought of all the miles I had yet to walk crossed my mind, and I said, "You know, even better than aspirins, I wish I had a good cup of hot coffee."

Once again his smile burst forth, this time revealing the gaps of several missing teeth. "Ah, yes," he commented, nodding thoughtfully. "A cup of strong coffee would be good."

His soft but direct response emboldened me, and I asked, "So, what brings you out here? I mean, I know the couple that lives here—did they hire you to shovel?"

His response was swift and to the point, as if he'd anticipated the question. "We're staying at a shelter downtown. That's my wife there, and my son," he added, nodding at the pair of shovelers. "When the snow came, the people at the shelter asked for volunteers to help dig out the old folks." He turned his head toward his truck and pointed to it with his lips. "I drive that old pickup, so I said we'd go."

He told me more, then, adding that they would soon be heading back up north. I assumed he meant to one of the Ojibwe reservations in northern Minnesota.

"It will soon be syruping time," he said, smiling. "My son is the best at boiling down the sap. Even the others bring their sap to him to cook. He knows just when the sugar is best."

The pride in his voice was obvious. I looked over at the tattooed face, but the young man kept working, even though I was sure he had heard his father's words.

"Well, I have to keep moving," I said. "Be careful working so hard. Don't hurt yourself in all this snow."

He laughed with his mouth wide open. "And I hope you find a cup of coffee!"

We parted ways then, him to his shoveling, and me to my route. I felt a little bad, though, about the way I had assumed he was looking for a handout. Whatever the facts were about his circumstances, he had been nothing but polite and friendly toward me, and he was doing what he could to help someone else. Right about now I wished there were several more shovelers just like him out there clearing off the sidewalks.

Most Minnesotans take a pragmatic approach to their snow shoveling—that is, to wait until the last flake is down to avoid working the job twice. Because this snowfall had continued into the late morning when most homeowners were off to work, I was left to tromp my own path through the yards.

With so many retired folks in the neighborhood, however, I knew the snowblowers would be out any time now. Wearing lined coveralls and heavy, felt-insulated boots, the elderly men are amazing to watch as they attack the drifts of snow. They clear off their own sidewalks and driveways, and most of the neighbors', too. They blow snow out of the alleys and clear the curbs in front of their houses. Their wives finish the job with a broom on the steps and stoop. I sometimes think that many of the wives come out simply to keep an eye on the men. Even with a five-horsepower machine doing the heavy lifting, operating a snowblower in the cold air can be tough on an old heart.

When the sidewalks and driveways are cleared, and all the neighbors are plowed out, the old men turn their snowblowers into the yards to open a narrow path for the letter carrier. Straight across the lawns they go, throwing massive arcs of snow, as well as branches, dead leaves, and clumps of sod. Each spring I encounter these same folks reseeding the lawns they destroy in the winter. On one of my blocks, the plowed pathway starts where I park my jeep and winds all the way to the far corner, connecting each house mailbox to mailbox. You can tell where one snowblower stops and another takes over by the various widths in the swaths they cut.

One year, when the snow was piled more than waist deep, crossing the lawn was like darting through the trenches in France in World War I. The neighborhood kids loved it, and, of course, so did I. I thanked one of the old-timers one day as he stood by his idling machine after clearing my path. The leather choppers on his hands vibrated and shook where they rested on the handlebars. His cheeks were bright red, his stocking cap stretched askew across his head, and his nose ran like an active four-year-old's. "By the time you get all these clothes on," he shouted, acknowledging my thanks, "and get the damn snow-blower running, a fella might as well make it worth the effort."

As if on cue, I heard a snowblower start up in the distance, and I rallied at the thought of walkways opening up soon. I decided to take my lunch break to allow them time to clear some trail. The snow-shoveling trio had long since loaded up and left. By the time my break was over, the whine of two-stroke engines filled the air. I drove my jeep over to the next street and began my trudging all over again. At some point a routine is set, and the blocks and the miles slowly fall behind.

The noise from the machines sounded like the amplified drone of a beehive, even more annoying than the scraping of shovels on concrete. But the sound signaled the opening of my paths and much easier walking. I waved at a man across the street running a snowblower. He walked through a miniature blizzard as the mounds of snow blew twenty feet or more into the air.

At the corner, I looked up in surprise to see the old pickup truck angling along the street. Deep ruts in the snow pulled it one way and shoved it back another. Behind the wheel was the old Ojibwe man, and I spotted the woman sitting beside him pointing at me. The engine revved and roared as the rear tires dug for traction. Pulling over to the curb would be impossible, so he stopped the truck in the middle of the deserted street and rolled down his window.

I stepped off the curb into the unplowed roadway. The old man was laughing, and his wife giggled beside him. At the far side of the bench seat, the young man leaned forward. Did I detect a hint of a smile on his face? With the truck stopped, he passed something to the woman, who gave it to the driver.

"*Aaniin niiji,*" the old man called as he handed over a tall cup of steaming hot coffee. The heat from the cup radiated straight into my cold hands. The earthy aroma engulfed me. My pleasure must have been evident, because they burst out laughing again.

"I have aspirins, too," he said, fumbling inside his coat.

"No, no. That's okay," I replied, holding up a hand. "This coffee is going to make my whole day."

And with that, the engine revved, the truck slid sideways, and they floated off down the snow-covered street like a boat over a froth-filled stream. Their laughter quickly faded away against the background racket of snowblowers. The young man waved at me through the back window, and I raised the cup to him in a salute of thanks.

The Lonely Pines

A woman on my route took the time one day to show me some black-and-white photographs of her house, the house she grew up in. A photo dated 1926 showed her two-story stucco home standing alone on the corner of the block where there are now thirty houses. Massive pine trees covered the surrounding open area. I could make out the woman, as a little girl, standing on the front steps. The street was no more than a dirt track. The family mailbox perched precariously atop a fence post near the roadway, and, in the foreground, a discarded axle lay mired in the mud. She told me that they had a milk cow and chickens.

The next photograph was dated thirty years later. All the trees were gone except two towering white pines in her side yard. Houses lined both sides of the paved street. Near the front door of her house was a small garden plot that I recognized immediately, because every spring her perennial bulbs come up in jumbled masses in that patch. Early in April I start checking for daffodils and crocuses to burst through the remaining snow, announcing with their vibrant colors the coming of spring.

Now, comparing the photograph from the 1950s to her house, it was amazing to see the changes that had occurred in a mere forty years. The garden patch had doubled or tripled in size. I stood back to take a closer look, and for the first time realized the two big pine trees were gone. "When did you cut down the trees?" I asked.

"I didn't." She showed me the next photograph, from 1965. Both trees were broken off at least twenty feet up their trunks. "They'd become too tall and top heavy," she informed me. "A big wind came through one night and knocked both of them down." She paused for a moment and smiled wistfully. "I used to lie in bed on summer nights with the windows open to listen to the breeze in the pine boughs."

"I bet that was nice," I said. "Sort of like being up north at a cabin on a lake. It must have been sad when they came down."

She nodded, then crossed her arms in front of her and held herself tight. Her gaze went up to where the virgin white pines had reached for the sky. "When my husband went off to war, he told me to listen for the wind in the trees. He said I'd hear his voice talking to me."

This surprised me, because I hadn't known she had been married. She turned her attention back to me when she sensed my confusion.

"We were married only a few months before he shipped out. I was pretty young," she added with a self-conscious smile. She was tall and slender, and it wasn't hard to picture her as a beautiful young lady.

"I know this sounds crazy; maybe I was just naïve and in

love, but sometimes at night I really did hear his voice in the trees. He told me about his plans and ambitions. He spoke of the family we'd have, and how the house would be full of children. He told me he loved me."

She slipped the photos into a pocket of her apron and looked out over her garden. "But I never saw him alive again. He died in the Pacific."

I suddenly had to sit down on her steps. Her story had sapped the strength from my knees. Bending over to pull weeds from among her tulips, she continued, "Of course, like I said, it was probably all in my imagination. It may have been my own words I heard." She told me about working her way through college and becoming a schoolteacher.

The intimacy of her tale emboldened me to ask, "But surely there were other men. You were so young, why didn't you remarry?"

The eighty-year-old woman sat down next to me. She moved with a dignified grace, smooth and languid. "Oh, there were some other boys around, I suppose." She slapped at my knee. "It wasn't like I never got asked out on a date, or anything."

I smiled and looked at her. A tear sat on her cheek. One slim drop, high up, perched just below her eye.

"But every night, you know, for twenty-some years, he'd come to me on the breeze in the pine trees. He remained faithful to me, how could I do otherwise?"

The loss of the trees took on a whole new meaning now. "I'm really sorry," I said. We sat quietly for a while with our thoughts. She never had the chance to raise a family, or grow old with a mate. In a way I felt angry with her husband for not allowing her to move on. Now she was all alone in her old age.

"I hired a man to cut up the trees and haul them away," she told me. "He said one of them had some rot, but the other one was totally solid. He figured the rotted one must have fallen and knocked the healthy one down."

I nodded. At least the trees had had a long life together.

"But that man was wrong," she continued. "I was awake the night they fell. It's true that the rotted one came down first. I heard it crack and break and hit the ground. I didn't even get up to look, because I knew exactly what had happened. I laid there for hours, listening to the wind for the rest of the night."

The tear had run down her cheek, chased by several more. With no family left, I wondered how many times she had told this story. It had the feeling of being the first.

"Just before dawn the wind died down. I didn't dare move. I listened with all my might. Then, I heard it. Just a creaking at first." Tears cascaded down her face. There were no sobs or sniffles, just a steady stream of tears.

"That old tree was dying," she said, turning a grim face at me. "It wasn't dying from rot, either. Soon the cracking got louder. When it finally fell, it landed on top of the other one. That's how I knew it fell of its own accord."

I didn't know what to say, so we just sat there for a few minutes. Before I left, she said, "They went together. Can you imagine how lonely the sound of the wind in one tree would be?"

Oops

One gorgeous fall day I came upon a small construction crew working in the front yard of a house on my route. The house itself was tiny. It sat way in the back of the lot, right at the alley. It was so small that there wasn't even a garage or an open place to park a vehicle. The owner drove a motorcycle for as much of the year as the weather would allow. He drove his Harley right through the front door and parked it on a sheet of plywood in the living room. When the snow came he holed up in his little house and tore the machine apart, rebuilding it and preparing for another summer of riding.

There wasn't any snow in the forecast yet, but Labor Day had come and gone weeks earlier, so we were getting by on borrowed time. In Minnesota, Labor Day marks the unofficial end to summer. It's a bittersweet time, because the State Fair runs through Labor Day, and while we look forward to spending a day at the fair, we know that when it's over the days will be getting shorter. Deck furniture disappears into garages, perennial gardens are cut back and buried under mulch, and frost covers windshields and lawns in the early morning hours. But until winter actually hits, we get to experience some of the most beautiful days of the year.

Minneapolis is built around dozens of parks and city lakes, connected by biking and walking paths, Minnehaha Parkway, and Minnehaha Creek. In the fall, this urban forest explodes into color. On sunny days the foliage glitters like billions of sequins caught in the light. The sky is a brilliant blue backdrop; the lakes reflect all the colors while their waters turn colder, day after day, until freeze-up.

Fall is a rather precarious time in the life of a letter carrier. I imagine the motorcyclist on my route feels the same way. Each year is different, with no way to predict how long the season will last. I've worn shorts while delivering mail in December and fought through freezing snow squalls in early October. In 1991, the Great Halloween Blizzard dumped nearly three feet of snow in less than forty-eight hours. For several days after that we went out two carriers to a jeep. By taking turns driving and pushing we somehow managed to get the mail delivered. That storm was one of the three weather systems that eventually collided over the Grand Banks in the Atlantic Ocean to create what became known as "the perfect storm."

Because of this potential for a quick descent into winter, we relish the mild, colorful days of fall. It's also why you'll detect a slight hesitation in the enthusiasm of a letter carrier for this time of year. We all know what's coming, and when it gets here, we'll be struggling with it for months.

But for this day, at least, we had stolen another one from

Old Man Winter. The little construction crew wore T-shirts and sunglasses; their tool belts were piled off to the side. I paused a moment to try to make out the nature of their project. They were working well away from the house, halfway to the street in the front yard. A shallow trench had been dug from the worksite to the corner of the house. I decided that was for electrical conduit, but what were they erecting way out here that would require wiring?

I studied the small pile of building materials, surely not enough for a garage. Besides, they would have poured a concrete slab first. My next thought was a shed for the motorcycle, but the lumber was solid white cedar. Not many people around here could afford expensive lumber like that for a shed.

Just then I heard the unmistakable rumble of a Harley coming down the street. I put the mail in the mailbox and turned to watch the motorcycle brake to bump over the curb. The owner slowly rode up the front sidewalk, looking at the construction crew as he passed. Pulling up to me near the door, he stopped and nodded a greeting.

The engine rattled and sputtered when he shut it off, like it didn't want the ride or the season to end any more than the rest of us. The sudden silence had a ring to it, and the biker sat astride his machine studying the work crew while our ears adjusted to the quiet. When he finally turned his long-haired, bearded head to look at me, I noted the oddest grin of confusion on his face. "What are they doing?" he asked.

I thought I must have misunderstood him. Now we were both confused, and we looked over the project and the front yard as if the answer might be hidden there, waiting to be revealed. I decided right then I wasn't going anywhere until I knew what this was all about.

The kickstand went down and a stiff leg swung over the seat. The rattle of a chain connecting his belt and wallet, and the creaking of his black leather jacket and chaps were the only sounds. The lead worker, clipboard in hand, approached and addressed the biker by name. "I just need your signature on this work order, and we'll be out of here by the end of the day."

The biker combed his thick fingers through his beard. Stalling for time, he took off his sunglasses and straightened out his long ponytail. His expression of confusion had deepened to a frown of downright bewilderment.

"What work order?" he asked.

"For your sauna."

"Sauna? You have to be kidding me."

The worker looked at the clipboard and repeated the name. "You bought it at the State Fair. It was a really good deal, too, with that last weekend holiday discount. You even instructed us to put it up in your front yard."

The biker looked around and threw out his arms. "I only *have* a front yard."

"Good choice then, sir. Now, if you'll just sign here."

"Wait a minute." The biker held up his hands and shook his head in disbelief. "You say I bought a sauna?"

They had forgotten all about me, so as long as I could refrain from laughing I got to be the proverbial fly on the wall.

"You paid for it with a credit card," the man said. "I have a copy of the receipt right here."

The biker studied the piece of paper. When he finally exhaled a big sigh, I figured he was beginning to succumb to the inevitable. "Sure looks like my signature," he said, looking up. "But are you sure it's supposed to be a sauna?"

The man laughed. "Yes, sir. And it's a large one, too. A barrel sauna with two bench seats."

"A barrel sauna?"

"Yep. Looks just like an enormous whiskey barrel tipped on its side."

The biker nodded, accepting his fate. "Oh yeah. I guess that does sound sort of familiar."

They worked their way back over the dates. He had bought it on the Saturday before Labor Day. "Well, I was there that day," he admitted. "Darned if I can remember buying it, though," he added, giving me a sheepish grin. "I've been carrying that credit card around in case of an emergency. What the heck am I supposed to do with a sauna?"

I'm pretty sure it never performed the function for which it was designed. It's still standing out in the front yard, though. The heating unit was dismantled that first winter and brought inside as an auxiliary heater in the small bedroom. A heavy padlock was added to the narrow wooden door. The bench seats hold all manner of motorcycle parts, from spare wheels to brakes, even whole transmissions. He told me once, "At least it's watertight. Things won't rust in there, and now I don't have to keep parts on the kitchen counter all winter long."

≡✉≡

I HAVE TO ADMIT that over the years I've made some mistakes when delivering mail. Probably not as outrageous as buying a sauna and not remembering it, but no matter how minor the infraction, mistakes are never appreciated. There are the little ones, like an envelope that sticks to another one so you never see it. You find it the next day, though, when it's still in the mailbox with a nasty note scribbled across it in big black letters, saying something like, "This goes to St. Louis! Can't you read?"

After being on the same route for an extended period of time, carriers learn to sort and deliver the mail by name, rather than address number. Any letter carrier will tell you that every day, on every route, there are pieces of mail bearing incorrect addresses. Sometimes it's a problem of dyslexia, or a computer glitch. Other times simply a wrong number, like an eight substituted for a nine. When that happens to the last number in an address, it puts the letter on the wrong side of the street. That happens daily. Delivering mail by name, then, prevents many misdeliveries.

One of the first things a letter carrier learns is to double-check to be sure he's on the right street and the correct corner. That sounds simple, and it's second nature when you do the same route every day. Substitute carriers, however, are often in a hurry, running way behind schedule in unfamiliar neighborhoods. Their mistakes are easy to understand. But substitutes aren't the only ones who have to pay attention. Several years ago I worked with two senior carriers who have since retired.

One day, both of them offered to work extra hours by delivering mail on a route whose regular carrier was sick. After first delivering their own routes, they drove to the second route later in the day. Halfway through a block they both stopped and looked across the street at each other. Obviously, one of them was on the wrong block. After a short pause they shrugged their shoulders and continued on their way. Neither carrier ever admitted to being the one who was wrong, but we laughed about that incident, and the unlikely image of two carriers going in opposite directions on the same street, for years afterward.

=✉=

As a substitute carrier, I often worked a route for several days for a regular carrier who was on vacation. Here's an obvious fact about mail volume: the wealthier the neighborhood, the more mail you carry, and this particular route received tons of mail. At each house I delivered eight or ten magazines and catalogs and a thick handful of letters. But mistakes happen in even the fanciest of neighborhoods.

As I meandered through this opulent streetscape of mansions and luxury sedans, I let myself be entertained by the exceeding beauty of the landscaping and architecture. Each property had its own varieties of trees and shrubs, many professionally manicured, but all of them in their full summer splendor. Cobblestone walkways allowed passage through gardens and patios.

One day I heard a faint cry for help. At first, I wasn't sure

I had heard it correctly because it was so quiet. But it came again, at regular intervals, seemingly out of nowhere. It was really unnerving, because the voice didn't sound upset in the least. If anything, it was a monotone of complete boredom. "Help. Help me please. If anyone can hear me, please help me."

I finally decided it was coming from the backyard of an enormous limestone and brick mansion. It took me a while to navigate my way through the gardens and gates and pathways, but eventually I found myself in the midst of a beautiful, quiet, terraced garden with a small waterfall and stream. A hobbit would have felt at home here, but I was uncomfortable. As far as I could tell, there was no one around. It seemed like I was trespassing in someone's little slice of Eden. I turned around to leave when I heard the voice again. "Say there, young man. Could you spare a moment to give me a hand?"

Looking around, I still couldn't spot the source of the voice. Then I heard, "Up here."

An older gentleman sat on a branch high up in a birch tree. His ladder had fallen while he trimmed dead limbs, and he'd been stuck up there for hours. Because the houses were spread so far apart, and most of the neighbors were at work or school, his calls for help had gone unanswered.

I found his ladder where it had fallen in the shrubbery. The man was very appreciative when I helped him down, as he could have been up there for several more hours.

While I knew that as a substitute carrier I needed to be paying constant attention to delivering the mail, it was impossible to keep my thoughts from wandering away in the peace and beauty of that quiet neighborhood. I think that's the reason I made such a ridiculous mistake a couple of days later. I chuckled to myself when I remembered the old man in the tree. Then I shoved two or three handfuls of mail down a slot and I heard it splatter across a hardwood floor. A horrible thought occurred to me and I tensed up with a rush of panic.

This couldn't be. I stepped back to look at the address over the entranceway. Sure enough, the owners were on vacation for at least another two weeks. The mail I had dropped down their slot belonged to the next house up the road.

As far as I knew, in my short career I had never made such a silly mistake. The first thought that came to mind was to simply walk away, skip the next house, and pretend that nothing had happened. If anyone should ask, I would plead total ignorance.

Head down, ignoring the beauty around me, I set off at a pace just short of a jog. By the time I began passing the next house, however, my conscience was getting the better of me. If that had been my mail, I reasoned, I would at least want to know that it had been misdelivered. With the large quantities of mail these folks received, they would have to be suspicious if a day went by without a delivery. I knew they would call the post office to ask about it. In the end, I decided my best recourse was to own up to the mistake and hope it would all blow over.

I climbed the imposing flagstone steps and stood before a massive solid wood door. Pushing the bell, I heard the stately report of chimes inside. The door slowly swung inward, and I was relieved to be met by a well-dressed young mother. A toddler peered up at me from behind her legs. The mother's broad white smile made me feel even more comfortable about my decision.

"May I help you?" she asked.

"Yes, well, you see," I stammered, "I'm pretty new at this job, and it seems I've made a terrible mistake."

The smile disappeared, and I was struck by how swiftly her expression went cold. My reaction was to quickly add, "Well, probably not so terrible as all that." I flashed her my best smile, but she wasn't willing to be reassured. I could tell that this was a big mistake. I should have played dumb, but now I had to go through with my confession.

"Do you have my mail?" she asked, very businesslike.

"Well, that's the problem. By mistake, I delivered your mail to the neighbor's house over there." She leaned out of the door to look down the road. "I just thought I should tell you," I added, "so you wouldn't wonder what happened to it."

When she again looked at me, her expression had gone from cold to frozen solid. Words came pouring out of me. "They're on vacation," I explained, "and I thought, you know, because you're neighbors, maybe you'd have a key or something. Some way to let yourself in to get your mail."

She didn't say anything, so I kept spewing nonsense. "I was hoping that maybe you were checking on their house for them, you know, like watering the plants or something. Maybe letting the cat out." I don't know where that came from. I had no reason to think they even owned a cat. "Or turning on different sets of lights at night. Sometimes neighbors do that for each other to make it look like someone's home."

I expected some sort of rebuke, but the icy vehemence in her voice startled me. "We haven't spoken to those people in over a year."

Those people? A form of rigor mortis infected my lips while my mouth hung open in shock. We stared at each other, and I knew she was waiting for me to solve the dilemma, but I had nothing to offer. Finally, I managed to croak out, "I'm sorry. I'm really sorry. I just thought you should know what happened to your mail."

For a long time after that I paid real close attention to my deliveries. When the regular carrier returned from his vacation, I told him what had happened. His response was much more casual. "Hey, don't worry about it," he laughed. "It's just the mail. They'll figure something out."

We joked about it, even coming up with the theory that the woman would have to go next door to get her mail, or the neighbor would bring it over to her, and perhaps they would rekindle a friendship. We never did find out what happened, but I kind of liked that idea—that maybe the neighbors would get along again because of my mistake. At least, that's my theory, and I'm sticking to it.

Undaunted Spirit

When one of the neighborhood gossips told me that Edith had been suffering from cancer for several years, I found it hard to believe. There are various signs and stages to the disease that are quite identifiable, but Edith had exhibited none of them. Retired and living alone, she seemed quite capable of taking care of herself and her two-story house.

"Are you sure?" I asked. "I mean, I see her almost every day. If she had taken chemotherapy or radiation, I would have known it."

"She's had it for years. It's either inoperable or she doesn't want surgery. But I know it's terminal."

It was one of those pieces of information I had tucked away in the back of my mind. I couldn't see how it could be true, and it was a topic that I felt uncomfortable asking Edith about. I mean, if she didn't tell me herself, but I asked her about it and it was true, she would know people were talking about her behind her back.

Besides, the way she performed chores around the yard

made a terminal illness unimaginable. She did all her own lawn mowing and raking. Using a ladder, she cleaned her gutters and washed the windows, although she admitted to me one time that she didn't much like climbing ladders anymore. She maintained birdfeeders and birdhouses and grew vegetables in a garden plot out back.

She seemed to have an endless supply of energy, quite unlike any cancer patient I had encountered before. When her own chores were caught up, she cleaned the neighbor's yard or swept the sidewalks. At other times I saw her on her daily walk around the neighborhood. After a couple years of this, the notion of Edith having cancer seemed ludicrous to me.

She told me one time about growing up dirt poor on a farm in Depression-era South Dakota. After World War II, she moved to Minneapolis with her husband to look for work and to raise a family. When the children were old enough, Edith joined her husband in the workforce, taking a full-time job in a factory. Her husband had died years ago, but her children and grandchildren were still in the metropolitan area.

The notion of her being sick had become no more than a distant memory to me when I ran into the neighborhood gossip again. She told me that Edith had taken a turn for the worse. The only reason I gave it any credence at all was because I hadn't seen Edith for a couple of days.

"She's in the hospital," the neighbor told me. "The cancer has spread all through her body. She probably won't be coming home."

For a day or two then I watched for Edith. It did seem as

though she had slowed down a bit in the last month. Even so, she had met me at the door almost every day. Now I wondered how difficult it had been for her to greet me with a pleasant smile and one of her wry comments while probably suffering great pain.

A couple of days later a pickup truck with South Dakota plates parked in front of Edith's house. An older gentleman fumbled with a bouquet of flowers while making his way up to her front door. This didn't seem like a good development.

"I'm Edith's brother," he said by way of introduction. The family resemblance was obvious. A tall, strong, capable man from rural South Dakota, he wore a leather string tie with a turquoise clasp over a western-style long-sleeve dress shirt. His face was deeply lined and tanned, accentuating a long white forehead. Only the cowboy hat was missing, and I thought perhaps he'd left it at home or in the truck out of respect. To my great relief, he told me she was coming home from the hospital later that day.

"So, what's the prognosis?" I asked, daring to hope for the best.

"Not so good. She's basically coming home to die." He explained that the extended family was coming together to care for her. It was a little awkward talking to him. After all, I had just met him, his sister was dying, and he had no knowledge of my friendship with Edith.

"Will you give her a message for me?" I asked.

"Sure."

"Tell her the mailman is thinking of her. I miss her and wish her well."

He smiled. "I'll do that. Thanks."

For a couple of weeks after that it was a merry-go-round of cars out front of Edith's house. I met three generations of her family, but I never saw her. Edith's brother told me that she had smiled when he gave her my greeting. "From her reaction, I can tell you must have been pretty good friends. I appreciate that." His expression clouded over, and he added, "She doesn't get out of bed anymore. I suppose it'll be any day now."

It still seemed impossible to me. Only a month earlier she had been meeting me at the door; a few weeks before that she was working in the yard. While I'm sure she cherished having her whole family around, I knew it must have been very hard on her to be bedridden. That just wasn't her style.

Her brother was staring at me. I didn't know what to say. My relationship with Edith had always been spontaneous and comfortable, full of teasing and joking around. Even though she was gravely ill, I thought that speaking to her would be easier right now than talking to her taciturn brother. I decided to pretend I was speaking directly to her.

"You tell Edith I'm waiting to see her at the door again." Bluffing a threat, I added, "Tell her I come by every day to deliver her mail, the least she can do is meet me at the door like she used to."

His expression was somewhat befuddled at first, but when he saw me smile, a conspiratorial grin broke out over his weather-beaten face. "By golly, I'll do it," he said with a wink. "I'll give her your message."

Walking away, I worried that my remarks had been disrespectful, that I had overstepped the bounds of civility. Arriving at Edith's house the next day, I found several more cars parked out front. Her brother, smoking a cigarette, stood on the steps watching me work my way down the block. A straw cowboy hat was pushed back on his head.

As I approached, he came down the steps and said, "She's been up since seven o'clock—baked muffins for the whole crew." He looked down at his boots and shook his head. "She didn't get out of bed for nearly a week, but after getting your message she's been watching for you all morning."

The fact that it was nearly lunchtime could have made that a humorous overstatement, but before he pulled the brim of his hat down I caught a glimpse of moisture around his eyes. Turning away, he nodded at the front door. "She's waiting for her mail."

Looking up, I was greeted by Edith's mischievous smile. Her whole family stood around her. I climbed the steps to hand her the mail, and she offered me a blueberry muffin in return. Her hand shook, and she'd lost a lot of weight, but that spirited gleam in her eye still flickered through the frailty. We talked as we always had, about the weather, and the lawn, and the birds at the feeders. And, just as always, we never mentioned the obvious.

She died two days later. Her brother thanked me for helping her go on such a positive note. "It was like a party around here—Edith herding her family around the house, baking desserts and keeping busy right up to the end. She just went in to take a nap and didn't get up again."

But, as I told him, it wasn't because of anything I did. It was her spirit and strength of character. It was all Edith.

Working It Out

My route runs through the middle of a blue-collar neighborhood with a wonderful diversity of residents. There are older folks and young, life-long bachelors and families with so many children it's hard to make a count, even when they're all playing in the yard. I meet people of every race and religion. There are a lot of friendly folks and a few crabby ones. Diligent, working class citizens, relaxed, retired seniors, and some people who don't work, don't want to work, yet somehow manage to survive off the system.

And there are always one or two that don't easily fit into any category. These are the people who attract no attention, are easily lost in a crowd, and disappear through the cracks of our society. One such character lived in a small house on my route. It took me years to learn his story. I pieced it together from bits of information offered by his mail, comments from neighbors, and snippets of conversation we had over the years.

Thomas was a chain smoker. I never saw him without a cigarette. His index fingers and long fingernails were stained a dull yellow. He wore the smell of cigarettes like an aftershave; it preceded him wherever he went and lingered in the air when he passed. His vocabulary and grammar were impeccable, but he needed to be spoken to first, as he would never presume to initiate a conversation. On those rare occasions when we did talk, he held his own on most topics, although I had to prod him regularly to keep him talking.

I assumed early on that Thomas got all his clothes at a second-hand store. He was tall and skinny, and his trousers were always several sizes too big, rolled up at the cuffs, and cinched tight around his waist with a narrow brown belt. He wore the same clothes for weeks at a time, which didn't improve his musty, nicotine-soaked aroma.

He wore thick, black-rimmed glasses. On someone else they might have been considered retro, or chic, but on Thomas were merely a degree or two beyond nerd. He was in his late forties, but he didn't work, didn't own or drive a car, and never learned how to ride a bicycle.

There was obviously something very wrong with Thomas, but I never heard him lament any aspect of his lot in life. His mail brought him a disability check as well as money from Social Security. In the summertime I usually encountered him sitting on the front steps reading a book. The first time we spoke, the book was *The Iliad*, by Homer. Having read it years earlier, I asked him how it was going.

"Oh, I've read this particular volume several times," he replied as if launching into a lecture. "It's far more engrossing than *The Odyssey*. After all, without *The Iliad* there wouldn't have been a Trojan Horse." He paused to scratch the top of his head, leaving a swatch of hair sticking straight up. It was apparent that he took his reading very seriously. "*The Iliad* is a great reference tool for understanding the Greek gods," he continued. "But everyone wants to read about the adventures of Odysseus, even though it's *The Iliad* that sets up his remarkable journey."

"Do you usually read a book more than once?"

As I would come to learn over the years, Thomas responded to the few things he confronted in life with an intellectual intensity that bordered on panic. Everything was a test, even my simple question, and he was like a game show contestant racing to throw out the correct answer. There wasn't much space left for common sense.

"When I deem it necessary, I'll read a book several times."

"And what have you uncovered in *The Iliad* that requires your reading it more than once?"

Thomas pushed his glasses further up on his nose. He had a bad habit of never looking at the person he spoke to. "It's that whole debate over the existence of Homer." He said this like it was a discussion everyone engages in from time to time. "At the very best, I'd give him credit for recording stories that had existed in the oral tradition for generations. But if you study the writing closely, you find variations in style, like you'd expect to find with more than one author."

Thomas set the book aside and scrunched his knees up tight. Looking at the sky above my head, he continued. "Please understand, I don't actually speak the language, but the term

Homer in Greek means hostage. In ancient times, the blind were often considered hostages, as in a hostage to their infirmity. So, I'm considering the theory that someone else may have written for a blind poet named Homer." He paused for a moment, gathering his thoughts. "In fact, it's just possible that Homer was a pseudonym of Plato. It becomes quite a mystery, especially when the original texts were written in ancient Greek. Who knows how the language has morphed after several layers of translations."

I considered Thomas in a different light after that initial conversation.

His mother was an odd character, too. She lived one hundred and fifty miles away in Duluth, a city in northern Minnesota with a port on Lake Superior. The first time I met her she breezed into town driving her big, flashy Cadillac. A sleek fur coat hung nearly to her feet. Despite her caked-on makeup and high heels, she looked ancient when viewed up close, which only made sense considering that Thomas was pushing fifty himself. Without help from her son, she carried two bags of groceries to the front steps. She then returned to the car to heft a large carton of books, which I helped her set on the landing. I recognized many of the titles, mostly classic hard covers, packed tight between layers of bubble wrap. There must have been a small fortune in books.

We introduced ourselves. I had seen her return address on letters she mailed to Thomas. She lived on London Road in the east end of Duluth. It was easy to envision this impeccably dressed woman ruling her domain from one of the large stone mansions overlooking the Lake Superior harbor, shipping canal, and lighthouse.

Thomas extracted two or three books at a time to bring inside. The entryway and living room beyond were a sea of books. I watched as he strategically placed each volume on a different stack, occasionally changing his mind to rearrange a pile, giving the distinct impression of having an order or system to the stacks.

Mother and son didn't have much to say to each other. He didn't invite her in, but she seemed to have no interest in lingering, anyway. I walked her back to her car. "That should be enough books to keep him busy for another month or two," she said without looking back.

"Your son is a prolific reader," I offered.

"And a prolific smoker, too," she added with sarcasm. "I'm surprised he hasn't burned down the house and all those books with his damn cigarettes."

At the door she paused to look at me. She carried herself with elegance and poise. Her hair was long, pure white from age, and piled high on her head in a hairdo more common to an earlier era.

I said, "His smoking aside, Thomas is a brilliant man. Where did he go to school?"

Pulling the door open, she hesitated, resting a gloved hand on the top of the doorframe. "We sent him to the finest schools in Europe. Did you know he's fluent in four different languages?"

Of course I didn't know that, but I was so surprised by the information that I blurted, "Well, he doesn't know ancient Greek."

She gave me a puzzled look, ignored my stupid grin, and continued. "He was born in Germany. My husband was a diplomat for the U.S. government in Berlin at the time." She looked down at one of her heels, turned her foot sideways to get a better view, and added, "There was a problem with the birth. You may have noticed that Thomas struggles with the details of his life."

What a strange way to put it, I thought.

On another occasion, I found Thomas pacing along the side of the house. As I watched him muttering to himself and gesticulating at a nonexistent audience, I wondered what caused him so much distress.

"Hello, Thomas."

It took a moment for him to come back to himself and recognize me standing at the corner of his house. He broke off pacing and approached me abruptly. "The city is going to fine me if I don't clear the brush from around my garage. I have to paint it, too."

The look on his face expressed fear and panic, not the anger I would have expected. As far as I could see, his whole yard was a disaster area. A paint job seemed like the least of his problems, considering the house had been in need of a new roof for the last five years. He handed me the letter.

"Says here you have six weeks before they take action." Thomas crowded up next to me to see the letter. I was certain he had read it hundreds of times already. The rank aroma of cigarettes and body odor wafted over me. Stepping aside, I said, "Why don't you clear some of that brush away and see what kind of a job you're looking at? It probably won't be too bad. It's a small garage."

Thomas was incredulous. "I don't even use the garage!"

"But it's yours, and it's on your property."

"It's my mother's property."

"Regardless, your neighbors don't want to look at the mess back there. It's an eyesore."

Thomas peered at the neighbor's house, suspicion in his eyes.

"Not necessarily that particular neighbor," I quickly added. "Just, you know, the neighborhood in general. Folks around here take good care of their belongings, and they don't want to look at a mess like that all the time."

Thomas surveyed the houses down the block like it was the first time he had ever noticed them.

"Just cut back some of that brush. You have lots of time. Do a little each day."

I left him with that thought. The next day I found him sitting on the steps, a cigarette burning a black smudge in the concrete next to him, his nose buried deep in a book. "How did the brush cutting go?" I asked.

He looked up, startled, fumbling to put the cigarette in his mouth. Holding up a shaky hand, he displayed several band-aids and dried blood on his fingers.

"How did that happen? Are you okay?"

Thomas was in a high state of agitation. I don't know if it was due to the bloodied fingers, the anxiety of a seemingly impossible task, or anger at the city for thrusting this ordeal on him. Whatever the reason, Thomas was too distraught for words.

I helped myself to a walk in the backyard. There wasn't much of a dent in the tangle of buckthorn and vines clinging to the garage. I spied a kitchen knife, and then a scissors, lying in the grass. I should have known he didn't have the tools, much less the capability, to cut back the brush.

Over the next few weeks I kept an eye on the backyard. The bushes appeared to be having a good summer of growth. Thomas didn't show himself, but a couple of times I thought I saw movement behind the blinds in the front room. Finally, just a few days before the city inspectors were due to return, I again encountered Thomas on the front steps. He wasn't reading, but sat watching me approach. The smoke from the cigarette dangling from his lips gave him a ghostly appearance. Maybe it was more wretched than ghostly, but either way, I found myself feeling sorry for him. Without being invited, I sat beside him on the steps.

"What, no book today, Thomas?"

No response. Smoke blew straight out from his puckered lips. I could feel the tension around him. He wasn't so much smoking the cigarette as sucking the very essence out of it. I had a hunch as to what was bothering him, so I asked, "Have you thought about hiring someone to work on your garage?"

When he replied, his voice was strained, edgy, almost falsetto in timbre. "Are you crazy? It's too much money. I can't afford that."

"What about your mother? Won't she help pay for it?"

"She told me to deal with it," he sneered. "She said it's my problem."

We sat for a few moments. When he reached for another cigarette to light off the one still burning, I had to get up and move away. His hands shook as he performed the habitual lighting ceremony.

"Have you ever had a job, Thomas?" I asked. I wasn't trying to be mean, it was a question I had wanted to ask for a long time. I didn't expect him to respond, so when he began talking I sat down again to listen.

The first words out of his mouth were the name of a huge market research firm in downtown Minneapolis. "I managed the accounting department. All receivables and expenses went through me. There were two whole walls lined with filing cabinets. Even though I had four assistants, I knew the status of each and every account. More than two million dollars worth a year."

I was shocked. If it had been anyone else I would have burst out laughing, but Thomas wasn't the joking sort. Smoke billowed around him again when he stopped talking. Time for some prodding.

"How long ago was that?"

Without hesitation, he responded, "Over twenty years ago. Before all the computers and everything. We lived in an apartment in Uptown back then."

"We?"

"Catherine and myself. She was my girlfriend, but it didn't last."

This was too much. An executive position was a stretch, but a live-in girlfriend, too? "Hmm. Thomas, what happened to the job?"

"I had to resign. The board was reluctant to let me go, but the pressure was too much for me."

"I suppose having responsibility for all those accounts, not to mention all that money, would be a little nerve-wracking."

"On the contrary, the position was perfect for me," he countered. "When I started, there were two rooms stacked to the ceiling with boxes of papers and files. I went through every one of them, cataloged and filed everything. After it was all organized, one of the rooms became my office. My desk was a huge antique wooden credenza, and I had a conference table with chairs. When anyone in the firm needed client information, they came to me."

Again the smoke plumed forth as we sat in silence. It was such an unlikely story, but I couldn't imagine Thomas lying to me. He had me hooked, though, so again I prodded. "Why did you quit, Thomas?"

This time it took a while for him to respond. "I went to the hospital."

We were obviously entering a dark part of the story, so I backed off and let him smoke. When he began talking again, it was of his own volition.

"I could have returned to work. They offered me my old position back, even after being out six months. I tried, but I couldn't sleep, and I didn't want to return to the hospital."

"Why couldn't you sleep?"

"Because I didn't want to miss my bus."

I didn't know what to think at that point. It seemed I was misunderstanding something. "So you miss your bus. Take the next one."

"My bus was the 7F. Every day it stopped in front of my apartment at 6:28 AM. It arrived at my office right on time."

"But surely there were other buses that stopped at your corner."

"Not the 6:28 AM 7F," he replied, wagging his head in the negative. "For a while I got up early to wait outside to be sure I didn't miss it. And you're right, dozens of buses went by, but not the 6:28 AM 7F."

This was just too much. "You got up early to watch buses go by until yours came along? How early did you go outside?"

"Four o'clock. Sometimes three o'clock when sleep was impossible. I always worried that my alarm clock would malfunction."

"You could have just used two clocks," I commented.

"What if the power went out?"

Ah, the logic of an obsessive-compulsive mind.

"At the end, I couldn't sleep at all. I kept checking the alarm, resetting it. Did I hit the wrong button? Better check again. Did I just hit PM rather than AM? Better check." Thomas paused to crush out his cigarette. "They said I had a breakdown. Catherine left when I went into the hospital. I can't blame her."

It was such a pathetic story, yet I couldn't help feeling sorry for him. His mother's words regarding his inability to cope with the details in his life came back to me. After that, it didn't seem appropriate to prod him about Catherine, or why his mother bought the house for him, or even the bushes lining his garage. I had learned enough for one day.

One more time I wandered into the backyard, wishing there was something I could do to help. The kitchen knife and scissors still lay in the weeds where I had spied them weeks earlier. I stepped out to the alley to get a better view of the garage. It was very small, but appeared basically sound under the flaking and peeling paint. I looked up and down the alley, and then an idea hit me.

"Thomas," I called, returning to the front yard. "Maybe I can help with your garage problem."

"What do you mean?"

"Let me think about it. We'll talk tomorrow, okay?"

I'm pleased to report that my plan worked out splendidly. In fact, the arrangement still exists. And the answers to some of my questions regarding Thomas's personal life have slowly been revealed over the years. I even met the mysterious Catherine a time or two. But I'll just say that the next time I saw Thomas, I told him, "You know the house across the alley from you, the one with a sauna in the front yard? The guy drives a motorcycle. I had a talk with him this morning, and . . ."

The Wrong Place at the Right Time

I noticed another mail jeep as it passed through my route one day. There are only a couple of good reasons for another letter carrier to drive through my route. Occasionally, a nearby mail-man will swing by to join me for lunch. Or, if a carrier runs out of a postal form, it's much quicker to borrow one from another letter carrier than to drive all the way back to the station. But an experienced carrier would have known where to find me. This jeep had driven right on by, so I had to consider yet another possibility.

Substitute letter carriers can get miserably lost. It's common to confuse numbered streets with numbered avenues in South Minneapolis. Once or twice a week a passing motorist stops me and asks for directions. Knowing that, and because I hadn't gotten a good look at the driver, I finished the block and set out to find the wandering jeep. I didn't have to search far. Just two streets over I spotted it at the curb near the far end of the block. Pulling in behind him, I parked and walked up to talk. I had never seen the carrier before.

"Can I help you?" I asked.

He pulled out a postal ID badge and an Inspection Service photo ID. Glancing at them, I also noted his solid build and his fresh, new uniform. His postal cap also looked new, without a sweat stain or bend in the brim.

"What's going on?"

He nodded at a house near the alley up on the next side street. It was difficult to see from here, but when he read off the address, I knew exactly which house he meant. "Do you know who lives there?"

"Of course," I replied. I told him the resident's name and added, "He's lived there at least ten years. Now, what's going on?"

"Nobody else in the house?"

I hesitated. As letter carriers, we're not supposed to give out names and addresses of patrons. In my whole career I remember doing so only once. A young mother driving a minivan with two small children inside asked me where a particular family lived. "I must have written down the wrong address," she said. I told her where they lived, but added, "Don't tell them you heard it from me." Shortly thereafter, I saw them all out in the backyard playing, so I knew it was okay.

But this guy had identified himself as a postal inspector, a member of an elite cadre of law enforcement. Working behind the scenes, they often make the FBI look like kindergarten monitors. I had never seen an actual agent before, but now one sat in a jeep on my route. Something big was going down, and he needed information that I could give him.

"Does anyone else live in the house?" he asked again.

"Not that I know of. I've seen a woman a few times, but she's a visitor. At least, she doesn't receive any mail there."

"Is her name Terry?" he asked, crisp and businesslike. Then he answered his own question. "She's at work. Verified."

"Okay, well, really, I don't know anything about her." I found it irritating that this outsider knew something about my route that I didn't know.

"Any children in the house?"

I shook my head. "Nope."

"How about pets? Does he have any dogs?"

"No. It's just him. Listen, can you tell me what's going on?"

"Do you think he's home right now?"

I looked at the house. The man's pickup truck sat outside. "He's a construction worker," I said. "But you probably already know that. Sometimes he takes time off when the work slows down. Looks like he's home, that's his truck."

"Well, okay then. Thanks for your help."

"But, can't you tell me what's going on?"

"No time." Looking at his watch, he added, "We're going in."

"We?"

The jeep started up and he edged away from the curb. Looking around, I spotted a squad car on the next block and two policemen stalking up the alley. Across the street sat two unmarked cars. And, now that I really looked, a man standing on the corner didn't belong there. I sure didn't recognize him from the neighborhood. I also caught furtive movements in the backyard.

Parked in front of the house now, the inspector walked briskly up the sidewalk. Under his arm he carried an Express Mail packet, which required a signature. That is, if it was real.

From the safety of my jeep just half a block away, I had a good view of the proceedings. He made a dashing, fit, competent-looking letter carrier as he bounded up the steps. Then I realized that what had looked like a stocky, muscular build was actually a bulletproof vest under his postal shirt. Without hesitation, he rang the bell.

After a minute the resident appeared in the doorway. The inspector greeted him with a smile. He held out the Express Mail envelope, indicating where it needed to be signed. I watched as police officers crept along the side of the house. Across the street, the plainclothes cop sauntered closer.

The whole thing happened very quickly. The inspector held out a pen. When the resident finished signing and handed the pen back, the agent grabbed his wrist and yanked him outside. The man fell down the steps. Within seconds he was face down on the lawn, the inspector grappling to handcuff him. Cops surrounded the scene, guns drawn. And they kept coming—out of neighboring yards, a cargo van, and an unmarked sheriff's car I hadn't noticed.

Afterwards, as the inspector removed his vest, he filled me in on what had happened. The guy had been dealing heroin and methamphetamines for quite a while. This was news to me; in all the times I talked to him, I had seen no sign of illegal activity.

"Didn't you notice all the Express Mail envelopes?" the inspector asked. "Haven't you ever wondered why he'd be getting so many of them?"

He was right. Now that I thought about it, I remembered delivering overnight packages on several occasions. I must have unwittingly facilitated his entrepreneurial escapade.

The inspector told me that the man's sister supplied the drugs, shipping them through the mail from Texas. Random searches by drug-sniffing dogs had alerted the Inspection Service.

"She didn't want the drugs sitting around in the mail stream, so she sent them overnight delivery. I'm sure there was plenty of profit to cover the extra expense."

His cell phone rang while we spoke. The authorities in Texas told him their bust had gone off perfectly down there, too. Inspectors had coordinated their raids so neither end would be suspicious or forewarned. I, for one, was totally impressed.

EVERY WEEK I RECEIVE requests for information on specific residents from government agencies and law enforcement. These are form letters sent out by county or state authorities seeking the whereabouts of bail jumpers or deadbeat dads.

After the 9/11 terrorist attacks, I arrived at a nearby National Guard unit to retrieve their outgoing mail and was confronted by a troop of M-16–wielding guards. These fellows were not kidding around. I was taken to the mailroom building under armed escort, but I wasn't allowed to leave my jeep.

"Hey," I confided to the nearest soldier, his rifle aimed at my head. "You know, this mail doesn't mean all that much to me. I'll be happy to leave if you want."

Instead, soldiers collected the sacks of outgoing mail and piled them in my vehicle. While I was never in real danger, it was unnerving to have at least a dozen fully automatic weapons pointed at me.

That little adventure occurred because I volunteered to go to the airbase on a day the regular letter carrier had off. I didn't think to ask, and nobody warned me of the heightened security. I haven't made that mistake again, but sometimes a situation just develops, and by simple coincidence the mailman wanders right into the middle of it.

One of those uncomfortable incidents happened to me on another route. The regular carrier needed to get off early on Saturday, so we split up his afternoon deliveries. It was a gorgeous day, with no reason for me to expect trouble. I even left the station early to begin my rounds. I decided to work the mail off the other route first, while still fresh, with the idea that many people wouldn't be out yet, and their dogs would still be inside. I would return to the familiarity of my own route later in the morning. By walking a little quicker, I intended to make up lost time and finish my route close to my regular schedule.

I launched into the challenge of searching for unfamiliar mailboxes and house address numbers while avoiding discarded garden implements, all the while watching for missorted letters and listening for stray dogs. The plan worked well for several blocks. Then, while fingering through mail for the next house, I heard voices rising in anger. A man and woman, really upset, were screaming at each other. I paused for a moment to listen. The racket was coming from the open window of the house in front of me.

Slowly, then, I continued my approach, hoping they would break off the fight if they saw me outside their window. After only a couple steps, however, the yelling resumed even louder than before. Then I heard a sharp "WHACK!"

Again I stopped. For a moment there was silence, but the slap seemed to resonate in the air. The man started yelling again, and I inched closer. When I reached the bottom of the steps, I heard an even louder "SMACK!" He shouted names at her, his voice quivering with rage.

I was alone and totally exposed on their walkway. No doubt the man could hurt her. He probably already had. I couldn't just leave, and maybe there wasn't even time to go for help. With my heart pounding, I searched for the appropriate thing to do. In a daze I climbed the steps.

From the landing, in the breaks in his vicious tirade, I heard whimpering, sniffles, and moans. The man's voice grew louder again. He sounded big, and as vulnerable as I felt standing out on their front steps, I couldn't imagine what the woman was going through inside the house. The street and yards remained vacant. I felt the tension building, another explosion imminent. Then my hand reached out and pushed the doorbell.

"Oh crap!" I cursed, realizing what I had done. "Now what am I supposed to do?"

Except for the banging of my heart in my ears, there was

complete silence. Again I searched the block for help, but found no one around. Had the neighbors heard the fight? Had someone already called the police?

When I turned back to the house, the inside door swung open, and a huge man in boxer shorts and T-shirt looked out at me.

"What!" he demanded.

"Umm . . ." I looked at the stack of letters in my hand. "I'm really sorry to disturb you," I stalled. "Really I am, but you see, I'm new on this route. I've never been here before, and I just wondered if this mail belongs to you." I shoved a handful of letters at him.

It was the lamest excuse imaginable, but under the circumstances, it was the best I could do.

"What?" he retorted, angry. "You can't be serious."

I detected a shadow of movement behind him. Again I thrust the letters at him to keep him distracted. "Would you just check a couple of these names?"

He opened the screen door to grab the letters, but didn't come outside. While he haphazardly rifled through the stack, I heard the side door quietly swing open and shut. Apparently, he couldn't hear it from inside.

"Well, thanks," I said, breathing a sigh of relief while retreating down the steps.

"What? Hey, wait a minute," he called, but I was already cruising across the front lawn. Just in time, too, to see the neighbor's side door slip shut.

"Come back here!" he demanded. "Not all this is mine."

I flicked a carefree wave over my shoulder behind me. "Thanks again," I called.

Out in the open, away from their front stoop, I felt much safer. I knew he wouldn't make an issue of things out in public. My adrenaline was pumping, though, and for a while I probably set speed records for delivering the mail.

I've never been back to that block, never met that woman. But I kept myself informed through the regular carrier. He ran into her a few weeks later when she returned with friends to move out. She had a court-issued restraining order against her husband. Soon they divorced, moved their separate ways, and sold the house.

I would like to thank that woman. She kept her wits, did exactly what she needed to do—and her escape permitted mine. She didn't look back, and for that I'm truly grateful.

A Nod and a Grin

Jackson was a quiet young man on my route who grew up in a house full of girls. He had a modest nature, but his sisters were not shy at all. Every day in the summer the girls argued over who would get the mail from me to hand deliver to their mother, grandmother, or one of their aunts. The matrons lined up chairs across the front porch and read magazines or knitted while keeping an eye on the children playing in the yard. I suspected that in summertime, with all those bodies residing under one roof, the front yard was welcomed as another room to spread out in. While he often took part in their fun and games, it seemed to me that Jackson more often stood on the sidelines, quietly observing his sisters, sometimes smiling at their boisterous antics.

The family claimed a Dakota Indian heritage, and I think Jackson was the second oldest among his siblings, but there were cousins who lived with them from time to time so it was difficult to place him in the group of children. He always watched me as I delivered their mail, and something in his intense gaze made me wonder if he saw in me a role model. After all, there had been no father figure in the household for all the years I had known them.

An uncle moved in and out of the house several times over the years. He was a decent fellow, but down on his luck in the job department. The entire family was courteous and polite. The young girls always said please and thank you when I gave them the mail, and the adult women usually had a friendly greeting or comment for me as I passed. I never heard a bad word or a voice raised in anger.

I'm sure they struggled financially. They didn't own a car, and they all went shopping together, trooping down the sidewalk to the bus stop like a family of ducks. Over the years I noticed several articles of clothing passed along from child to child, and they received government checks. Even so, every year during the Letter Carrier's Food Drive, I picked up a full bag of groceries from their front porch for the food shelf.

Their yard was always littered with toys and tricycles and discarded clothing. They had an ancient rotary lawn mower that the children teamed up to push over the grass, but it didn't help the constant clutter or bare spots that erupted each summer under the children's play. I overheard a neighbor refer to them as "that trash down the block," but I didn't see them that way. The mother, aunts, and grandmother were committed to and involved in every aspect of the children's lives; they played together and took care of each other better than many of the "neatest" families on my route.

One day I came upon Jackson playing football in the street

with his uncle and older sister. He was about twelve years old, wearing an extra-large Minnesota Vikings jersey that hung to his knees. He was nearing that gangly age, not a child anymore but not quite grown up yet, either. I was impressed with his speed. His uncle was faster, of course, but Jack was beginning to show his stuff. On a whim I joined them.

"Hey, Jackson," I called. "You know how to run pass patterns?"

He nodded, flipping the ball to me when I held my hands up for it.

"Think you can beat your uncle?"

Dropping his eyes to his feet, he meekly shook his head.

"I bet you can," I said. Turning to look at his tall, rangy uncle, I called, "How about it? One play. I'll be quarterback, you cover Jack."

"You're on," he answered, grinning. "Bring it on, Little Jack!"

I set the football in the middle of the street and laid my mail satchel near the curb. When I pulled Jackson back into a huddle, his sister followed. "What do I do?" she asked.

"You're the hiker," I said. She wrinkled her nose so I quickly added, "It's a really important job. If the hike is no good, I won't be able to pass it to your brother, and we only get one chance."

That seemed to mollify her. She nodded at me, and then aimed a grimace of determination at her brother. "You better catch the ball, Jackson."

I held my hand out in front of them in the time-honored tradition of diagramming a pass play on the palm of my hand. "You know what a buttonhook is?" I asked him.

He shook his head. His eyes were glued to my hand. I could see his excitement as his tongue flicked over his lips while he rocked from foot to foot. "How about a fly pattern?"

Another shake of the head. Again the darting tongue and pacing in place.

"Okay, then this is how it works. Your sister hikes the ball to me. You run as fast as you can for five steps. Count them as you go. On the fifth step turn around and yell for me to throw the ball."

I drew all this with an index finger on my palm. The children watched my finger move, as if hypnotized by the sequence of wriggles and waggles.

"I'll fake a pass to you," I continued, "then you take off down the street as fast as you can run." My finger drew a straight line off the end of my fingertips. "Just run, Jackson, for all you're worth. The next time you look back, I'll be launching a long bomb to you. Got it? It's called a buttonhook and fly. It'll work, Jackson, if you sell the fake."

He nodded, but when we broke huddle he started out the wrong way down the street. He turned around when his sister called him. Holding the ball and laughing, she said, "Where are you going?"

A drop of doubt entered my thoughts then, but I decided he was just concentrating too hard on the route he had to run.

"Come on, little boy," his uncle taunted. Jackson ignored the remark and took his place next to his sister. I had a notion he was doing some growing up right there in the middle of the street. The other children lined up at the curb to watch the play, while the older women sat forward on their porch chairs, leaning on the railing to see what the mailman was up to. Jackson snuck a peek at the house to be sure they were watching.

"Hike!" I called, and the ball sailed high over my head.

I backtracked enough to grab it, but by the time I looked up, Jackson's sister was already yelling, "Throw the ball!" As I stepped forward into my fake pass, Jackson shouted, "Throw it!" His uncle charged forward to block the pass. On his final lunge he bellowed at his nephew to intimidate him, but by then it was too late. Jackson turned on his heel and flew down the street. My bomb floated high and deep, spiraling between the branches of overhanging boulevard trees. The uncle gave chase and quickly closed the gap. I held my breath while Jackson ran all out. When he caught the ball and safely tucked it away, a chorus of cheers erupted from the front yard. His mother and grandmother jumped off the porch, high-fiving each other while screaming like we'd just won the Super Bowl.

Jackson tried to act nonchalant about it, but it was impossible for him to keep the huge grin off his face. Trotting back to us, he modestly looked down at the street or off to the side, secretly stealing a glance at his mother. The joy on his face made the sixty seconds I had spent in the street well worth the time. After that, whenever I encountered the family in the front yard, Jackson and I exchanged conspiratorial nods and grins.

=✉=

AS THE YEARS PASSED I watched Jackson grow into a handsome young man, through the awkward voice-changing and acne years. He was small for his age, but very fast, and it was hard to miss the glint of self-awareness and intelligence in his pitch-black eyes.

His uncle came and went a few more times before finally moving out for good. I had a few short conversations with Jackson over the years, mostly to ask him about school, and to encourage him to work hard at it. I don't believe my urgings were necessary, however, as his mother and grandmother kept a pretty tight rein on the kids.

He played baseball for the high school team. I asked him about it one time when I came upon him in his baseball uniform playing catch with his sister. "We're not very good," was his comment on the team.

"Oh, come on, I bet you're better than that."

"No, really, we always lose."

His sister interjected, "His stupid coach won't let him play."

"Shut up," Jackson ordered.

"Well, it's true," she persisted. "And it's not fair. You lose every game anyway, what difference does it make? He should let you play."

Jackson ignored her. I was stuck for something to say. My thoughts were torn between the warmth of his sister's loyalty, and the cold shadow of an injustice that I could only guess at. Was he on the bench because of his size? Was it a racial thing? It certainly couldn't be poor academics, not with the way his mother rode herd on him.

"Do you make it to all the practices?" I asked.

Jackson nodded, but again it was his sister who replied. "Oh, yeah, he goes to practice. I should know, too, because I go to all of them with him."

"That's only because Jeremy is there," Jackson said, rolling his eyes at his sister.

"Shut up!" she yelled, throwing the ball at him.

"Practices are important," I said in my best adult fashion. The notion of being a mentor came back to me. "That's where you learn. Even if you're not playing, practice hard. Use the time to develop your own skills. Especially in batting practice. Learn all you can. If you work hard at it, the coach is bound to notice you. The playing time will come if you keep working at it."

The baseball fields where Jackson's team practiced and played their home games that summer were near the neighborhood. Sometimes in the evening, when I was out riding my bicycle, I swung by to see if the team was out there. When they practiced, I stopped for a few minutes to watch, but when they played games, I usually hung around for a couple innings. It brought back memories of when our own children were young and my wife and I lugged lawn chairs around to all the ballparks in South Minneapolis to watch their games.

I never saw Jackson in a game. Instead, he would put on a catcher's mitt and warm up the pitcher, or keep the infielders loose by playing catch with them on the sidelines. He was the only player on the team that didn't get playing time—at least, for the several innings that I witnessed, he never played.

The impressive thing about it, however, was that his whole family came out for every game. I even saw his uncle there one night. They took up most of a row in the short stand of bleachers. The younger children ran around playing in the park with friends while the older ones cheered on the team. I found their devotion to be amazing considering that what Jackson had told me was true: the team never won a game. The outcome usually wasn't even close.

When the players came in from the field to sit on the bench, Jackson often walked up and down the line high-fiving each kid. Even though he never played, he showed more team spirit than anyone else. I noticed his mother and grandmother laughing and cheering enthusiastically for the team's few good plays. Was I the only one having a problem with this?

Late in the season Jackson met me in his yard. "Are you coming to my game tonight? It's the last one of the season."

It's nearly impossible to say no to a kid who extends an invitation like that. Especially when it's a child I've watched grow up, one who is usually very quiet and unassuming. "Of course I'll be there," I replied. "Are you playing tonight?"

"I don't know," he said softly, looking at the toe of his shoe. "Coach doesn't announce the line-up until game time."

I looked up at the sunny, clear sky. It was hard to tell if he was lying about the line-up out of a false sense of optimism, or simply protecting his coach to avoid controversy. In either case, it would be a nice evening for a bike ride. "I'll be there," I promised.

The first two innings were completed by the time I arrived. The team was already several runs down, and Jackson sat on the bench. I locked up my bike and joined his family in the bleachers. For three more innings I watched the team fall further behind. Jackson continued his spirited efforts on the bench, however, cheering and encouraging his losing team-mates. It was the last game of the season, with no doubt as to the outcome. Come on coach, I ranted silently. Get everyone in the game!

As much as I disapprove of meddling adults at sporting events, I had finally seen enough. If I truly wanted to be a mentor, then my actions would have to speak louder than my words. In the sixth inning, when Jackson's team took the field, I quietly walked down to take a seat on the bench near the coach. Jackson was rounding up bats from the previous half-inning, lining them up by weight behind the backstop. The coach gave me a short once-over, then called out some adjust-ments to his outfielders.

I got right to the point. "How come you don't play Jackson?"

When he groaned, I thought it was directed at me, but he may have been reacting to another pitch lined into the outfield by an opposing batter. When things quieted down again, he said, "Everybody gets playing time." He didn't bother to look at me.

"For all the innings I've seen this summer, the kid hasn't taken one ground ball. Not even one at bat." I said this while watching Jackson behind the backstop shouting encourage-ment to his pitcher, but when the coach looked at me, I turned to meet his gaze.

"Who are you?" he asked.

"Jackson's mailman."

He snickered. "The mailman." Scanning the field again, he added, "Now I've heard everything. Like I said, Mr. Mailman, everyone gets playing time."

"Just saying it doesn't make it so," I retorted, standing up in front of him to block his view. "Here's another thing, Mr. Coach," I added with sarcasm. "I've watched him play ball and work out all summer. He's never missed a practice or a game. Hell, his whole family never misses a game. I've been coming down here after work to watch him play, and I have to say, your line-up choices really disappoint me."

The real disappointment I felt was in myself. A confrontation with the coach hadn't been on my agenda. As I walked away, I nodded at Jackson and he smiled, happy to see me there. Returning to the bleachers, I decided to wait out the remainder of the game. Maybe I would dream up some words of wisdom for Jackson when it was all over.

When the half-inning was completed, his sister pointed, shouting, "Look, Mom, Jackson's putting on a batting helmet!"

I couldn't believe it. Now he grabbed a bat, too, and stood in the on-deck circle taking practice swings. With no trace of teenage inhibition, he paused to grin and wave at us.

The other team had a new pitcher, a big kid who threw hard. He struck out the batter before Jackson on three pitches. I watched the coach sit back wearily and shake his head as Jackson stepped into the batter's box. Digging his cleats in, rocking from foot to foot and licking his lips just as he'd done in our football huddle, I saw the signs of concentration on Jack's face.

A NOD AND A GRIN

"Come on," I whispered. "Take a pitch or two, get your timing down. This guy is really throwing heat." His mother and sisters screamed and cheered, yelling loud enough for people to turn and look at us.

Jackson ignored my silent pleas and swung wild at the first pitch. He crushed the ball with a line shot that cleared the first baseman's head before the kid could even react. The ball sliced off into the right-field corner. Jackson shot out of the batter's box like a track star off the blocks, and our row in the bleachers lunged to our feet. "Run, Jackson, run!" his grandmother screamed in my ear.

He had a good view of the ball as he rounded first base. As fast as he was, it seemed like he accelerated on his way to second. Unfortunately, because he'd hit it so hard, the ball careened around the corner of the outfield very quickly. It ricocheted up to the right fielder before Jackson reached second base. I could see he had no intention of slowing down, even though the right fielder made a strong, accurate throw to the infield. Jackson cruised around second at top speed, ignoring the third-base coach's sign to hold up. I found myself jumping in place on the bleachers like everyone else, the excitement carrying us away. "Stop, Jackson!" I yelled. "Hold up!"

His batting helmet had long since blown away. I could see his tongue sticking out in concentration as he flew toward third base. He was so incredibly fast; all his movements were smooth and fluid. He seemed completely at ease, as if this element of great speed was a natural part of him, like the color of his eyes, or the tone of his voice.

He launched himself toward third base, diving head first as the ball arrived from the outfield. The umpire ran onto the field to get a clear view of the play. As the dust settled the umpire's arms flew out at his sides, and he yelled, "Safe!"

The bleachers erupted. The opposing coach got up to argue, but the umpire dramatically re-enacted his call. Flinging his arms straight out at his sides while directing his theatrics personally at the opposing coach, he sang out, "The runner is safe!"

We all laughed and cheered some more. When Jackson's grandmother jumped up to high-five me, I had to catch her to prevent her from crashing through the bleachers. Jackson stood on third base, his modesty once again in charge as he brushed himself off. A teammate ran his batting helmet over to him. Putting it on, he snuck a quick peek up at the bleachers. Just like the old days in his front yard, the familiar nod and grin came my way. Then his eyes moved down the row to find his mother. The grin broke out into an unabashed smile, and he waved at us, his black eyes shining with pride and joy.

Animal Kingdom

Coming across a certified letter requiring a signature, I climbed the steps to the house and rang the doorbell. From a thick bundle of letters I extracted the form that needed signing while searching my pockets for a pen. A young couple lived here, new on my route.

When the door opened, I greeted the young lady of the house. I held up the letter and said, "Here's a certified letter for you. It needs your signature. Looks like it's from the mortgage company."

She stepped outside. I smiled at her, admiring her friendly face, and then recoiled in horror. A huge albino python lay draped across her shoulders. It spanned from one outstretched hand, up her arm, through a wide loop around her neck, and down her other arm. It had to be eight feet long or more.

She laughed at my startled reaction. Introducing me to the snake, she stepped forward and asked, "Want to pet him?"

"No, thanks." I backpedaled down a step or two. I noticed the head of the snake weaving farther off her arm, aiming closer to my face.

"He's not poisonous or anything," she said. "He's really friendly."

From the lower step I handed the letter and pen up to her. The snake's face was even with mine, and much too close.

"I love this hot weather," she said. "When it's warm like this, I let the snakes out to exercise in the yard."

Snakes? As she spoke, the beady red eyes bobbed ever closer. Inching farther off her arm, the head performed a mesmerizing slow-motion dance. She handed the form back to me and asked, "Come on, are you sure you don't want to pet him?"

I shook my head. "I'm really not too fond of snakes."

Holding my breath, I looked the snake straight in the eyes, then reached out and snatched the form out of her hand. Back down on the sidewalk, I finally managed to breathe again. Not a day goes by without my searching that yard for runaway snakes.

BECAUSE I SPEND SO many hours outside every day, I get to see the whole gamut of wildlife that Mother Nature has to offer in the city. I've spotted pheasants, raccoons, and even a skunk. For a while, a yearling doe resided in the backyards of a block on my route. I enjoyed watching the homeowners adopt and protect that deer. When their small gardens matured, they live-trapped squirrels and rabbits and hauled them away, but they let the young deer eat all she wanted. Neighbors sat outside on lawn chairs, exchanging gossip while taking pictures of the deer as she grazed her way through their yards. With the coming of fall and the mating season, the doe suddenly disappeared. We all missed her, agreeing that her presence had made for an interesting summer.

With the resurgence of the wild turkey population in the Midwest, I've seen a couple of the big birds pecking through the neighborhood. For as smart and wary as they're alleged to be, they never show any concern over my presence.

There was another bird, however, that caused quite a ruckus several years ago. Big Ray, a letter carrier I worked with early in my career, stood six foot five, a gentle giant, but he somehow made an enemy out of a nesting robin on his route. He took to wearing a wide-brimmed bush hat to protect his head.

Big Ray's foe became quite a joke around the station. Even though it flustered him greatly, we teased Big Ray without mercy when he confided how this little bird attacked him with such ferocity.

I drove over to his route one day to see for myself. Sure enough, on the designated block, Big Ray donned the silly-looking hat. He walked cautiously, creeping through the yards like a soldier on patrol in Vietnam. He scanned the trees for the first sign of an ambush.

A tiny dark object suddenly hurled itself from the cover of a leafy branch. It zoomed within inches of Big Ray's head. He ducked into a crouch, rushing forward to the safety of an overhanging garage roof. Time and again the little kamikaze swooped in, and each time Big Ray ducked, flinging an arm up to protect his face.

From the safety of my jeep, I watched the big man pleading with that little bird to leave him alone. After a while, Ray sprinted ahead to the next house and then double-timed it to the cover of another garage roof. In this way he eventually escaped the bird's territory. For three weeks Big Ray endured the wrath of that robin, running the daily gauntlet, and providing laughs for the rest of us.

≡✉≡

EVEN IN THE URBAN SETTING of my mail route, it's possible to witness the day-to-day struggles of wildlife. Crows sometimes gang up, dozens of them, to harass an owl, chasing the raptor from tree to tree. Their racket can be heard for blocks around.

I stood on a patron's front stoop one day watching as a great horned owl attempted to elude his tireless pursuers. "Makes you feel kind of sorry for the poor guy," I commented.

Pulling his pipe from his mouth, exhaling a cloud of smoke, the elderly resident replied, "Well, I'll feel sorry for him for a while." Squinting at me through the smoke, he added, "But come sundown, the tables will be turned. Then it's payback time."

Hawks aren't nearly as rare as they used to be, and I saw a kestrel several times one summer. A letter carrier on a neighboring route saw the bird, too. Perched on a low branch, often right out in the open, it seemed the bird paid no attention to me at all. With his short forehead, intense eyes, and sleek profile, he was quite dapper. One day I watched as he suddenly darted off the branch, swooped between two houses, and lit into a backyard compost pile. When he returned, he clutched a mouse firmly in his talons.

=✉=

THERE'S ALWAYS PLENTY of wildlife around if one takes the time to look for it. Even so, the most bizarre occurrences, as well as the most frightening situations for letter carriers, involve man's so-called best friend.

Returning to the station one day, I found my supervisor on the phone with a neighborhood resident. She reported that stray dogs were harassing her letter carrier, and he appeared to require assistance. The carrier was a veteran named Mike, and even though we didn't think he really needed help, the supervisor sent me out to check on him.

This will be great fodder for some teasing, I thought. I was still grinning when I turned the corner and saw Mike's jeep parked down the block. He stood on the roof, a pair of rottweilers circling his jeep like sharks around a sinking boat.

I raced down the street, opened my window, and yelled at the dogs. They immediately turned on me. Creating the short diversion bought Mike enough time to scamper down off the roof and get in his jeep. With him safely inside, the dogs soon lost interest and wandered off.

Mike finished the route, and back at the station we gathered around to hear his story. He had seen the dogs coming for him from way down the block. He sprinted for the jeep, not sure if he could get there first. Fortunately, he won the race, but the dogs were so close he didn't have time to unlock the door. We laughed as he reenacted his attempts to jam the tiny brass key in the lock while two snarling, one-hundred-twenty pound carnivores closed in on him. At the last second he abandoned the effort and jumped up on the hood, the dogs lunging at his ankles. From there he climbed up on the roof to wait for the animals to leave or help to arrive.

≡✉≡

My scariest encounter was a run-in with a German shepherd named Timber. The young woman who owned him rented a small house on my route. I had plenty of warning about the dog, as almost every letter carrier in the station knew him.

The fellow I inherited the route from told me all of Timber's habits. Basically, the dog would either be in the house, posing no threat, or outside on his chain, in which case I should avoid the yard at all costs. A doghouse sat near the front door, and I had to ensure that Timber wasn't sleeping out of sight before entering the yard.

Fortunately, his chain was quite heavy. I don't think a tractor could have broken it. Also, Timber wasn't outside very often. Because Laura, his owner, worked days, he generally stayed inside all week. Every now and then I saw him on a Saturday, though, chained out by his doghouse. He watched me pass without so much as a bark. But a sinister intelligence glimmered in his eyes, and it gave me the creeps. He sat still as a statue, ears pointed straight out, sizing me up with a menacing, Hannibal Lecter–like stare.

I approached the yard that day looking for any sign of Timber. By now it was automatic, like putting on a seat belt. I gave a little whistle in case he was in the doghouse. I was so distracted that I didn't immediately notice Laura working in the front yard. She had just mowed the lawn and now sat out by the street pulling weeds in her small flower garden.

I walked up to her and handed her the mail. She was engaged in a friendly conversation with Pete, her next-door neighbor, who was working on his car in the driveway. I had never talked to her much, so I paused for a few minutes to chat. My fear of Timber was so ingrained, however, that I kept looking across the yard up to the house. His unknown whereabouts made me nervous, so I finally asked, "Where's Timber?"

"Oh, I keep him inside when I work out here. He gets so jealous and protective. He goes crazy if someone even walks by."

I caught a glimpse of him then, through the living room window. I relaxed, feeling I had survived yet another Saturday.

"He's a great dog," the neighbor interjected. "I take him for walks to get him some exercise. He's about the smartest dog I've ever met."

Laura added, "Timber is so strong I can't handle him alone on a leash. Pete is working to control him with voice commands."

Pete talked about his experiences in training dogs. "I really don't think Timber would hurt you," he concluded.

I laughed. "If you only knew how many times I've heard that one."

He tried to explain, and while he talked, I noticed how Laura looked at him. They were both single. It occurred to me that Pete wasn't really doing anything to his car, just using it as a pretext to talk to his neighbor.

Out of habit I glanced at the house again. Detecting movement through the bank of living room windows, my senses jumped to high alert. Ears straining, I heard Timber's muffled barks from inside. My heart began beating faster. I stepped aside, into the shade, to peer more intently through the windows at the other side of the yard. I could see the dog racing back and forth across the living room. Suddenly, he changed course and charged at the large, single-paned windows. When he leaped, he seemed to hang in mid air; then glass exploded, the screen flipped away, and Timber roared into the front yard.

Laura screamed, and I'm not too sure that I didn't do the same. The huge dog was on us in seconds. I've never used my dog spray, and I don't think it would have slowed Timber down anyway, but there wasn't time for that now. I ducked behind the woman, swinging my satchel off my shoulder to protect myself.

Timber came in low and fast, banking tight around Laura's legs. He almost knocked her down trying to get at me. Snarling, he lunged, and I whipped my mailbag between us just in time. He got a mouthful of the canvas bag and thrashed it from side to side while I desperately hung on to the shoulder strap. Mail flew everywhere. Timber's teeth punctured the satchel, and it became lodged in his mouth. I truly had a tiger by the tail.

All the while, Laura screamed, "He'll kill you! Oh, my God! He'll kill you!" She was hysterical, and her frantic yelling only intensified the situation.

I grabbed the back of her shirt to keep her between the chomping teeth and me. Pete yelled Timber's name, and for a split second the dog hesitated. I yanked the mailbag loose and prepared for the next assault.

When it came, the force of it startled all of us. Timber launched himself at me directly through Laura. She collapsed out of the way, knocked aside like a twig before a grizzly bear, and the snarling face lashed out at me. Staggering backwards, using the mailbag as a shield, I somehow avoided the snapping teeth.

Pete yelled again, and this time Timber stopped. When he turned to look at the neighbor, I ran for the street. He tried to come for me again, but Pete grabbed his collar, wrestled him to the ground, and with sheer strength and voice commands managed to hold him down.

I sat on the curb, shaking, gasping for breath. Laura lay on the lawn, sobbing. Mail was strewn across the yard, my mailbag lying in a heap near the sidewalk. Some of the neighbors had heard the racket and came out of their houses to see if we were all right. Pete sat on top of Timber, calming the dog with soft shushing sounds.

I had to report the incident. If Timber would launch himself right through a glass window, it wasn't safe to deliver mail there anymore. My supervisor backed me up. For a while, Laura rented a post office box. Why she kept that crazy animal I'll never know. From then on, when passing her house, I circled way out by the street.

Sometime later she moved. The house she bought was nearby, but far enough away to be off my route. I warned her new carrier about Timber. With the support of our supervisor, he insisted that she put a mailbox out by the street, and that seemed to solve the problem.

Years passed, and Timber grew old and frail. His carrier told me that the dog basked outside all day in the sunshine. He didn't bark at intruders anymore; in fact, he seldom even woke up from his nap when the mailman arrived. In his old age he was no longer a threat.

On a whim I stopped by one Saturday. Timber lay at the front door. He heard me approaching, but I'm not too sure he could see me. I carried my mailbag as a shield, though, just in case.

He let me sit with him. I petted his wide, heavy brow, while recounting for him our little incident of ten or twelve years earlier. Although I'm sure he had no recollection of me, sitting with the old warrior helped me close the book on that harrowing experience and come to terms with the fear that had so overwhelmed me that day.

It was hard to believe that this docile animal had once tried to kill me. But then, I had witnessed many changes in the neighborhood during the years since Timber's attack. Just a decade earlier, many of the residents had been retired, blue-collar, empty nesters. Now, young families were moving in, remodeling and updating the houses. There was more diversity. My daily passage through the neighborhood had been the one constant in all the changes.

Timber nestled his great head in my lap. We sat like that in the sunshine for a while longer. When I got up to leave, I left him with a dog biscuit and best wishes for a long and restful retirement.

Beware of Cat was designed and typeset by Percolator Graphic Design in Minneapolis. The type is Kingfisher, designed by Jeremy Tankard. Printed by Thomson-Shore, Dexter, Michigan.